T-Shirt Design Ideas Sketchbook for Merch By Amazon Sellers

Keep track of your Merch By Amazon t-shirt design ideas!

100 Pages of T-Shirt Design Templates

Sign up for Merch By Amazon at:

merch.amazon.com

T-Shirt Design Ideas Sketchbook for Merch By Amazon Sellers

Published by PBLLC Press, Rehoboth, MA 02769

First Printing, April 2016
Updated, April 2017

ISBN-13: 978-1530937042

ISBN-10: 1530937043

Printed in the United States of America

Reorder this book at:
Amazon.com/dp/1530937043

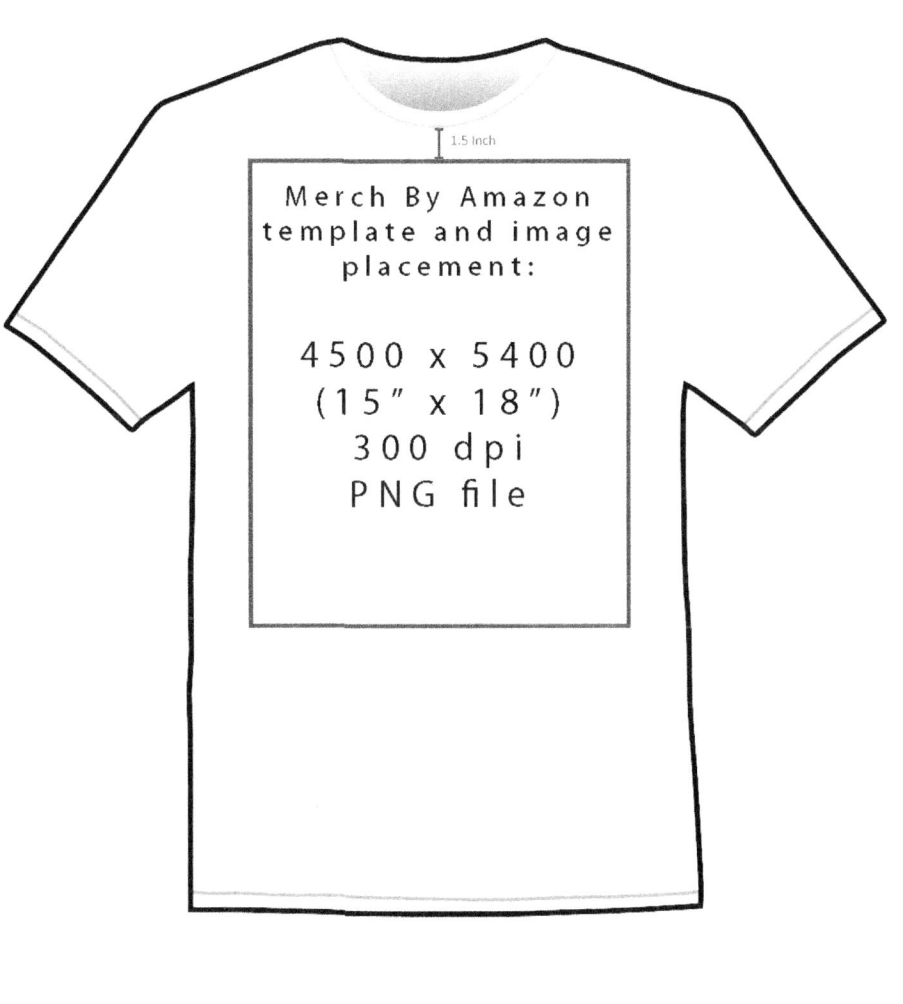

Official Merch By Amazon Resources

(Best Practices, Royalty Calculations, Content Policy, Tools, FAQ, Legal, & Downloadable Templates)

merch.amazon.com/resource

Merch By Amazon Resources:

MerchResearch.com
Search all Merch By Amazon designs by keyword as well as other print-on-demand sites, keyword tools, and more

MerchInformer.com
Simplified and streamlined Merch By Amazon research tool (use code chris20 to save 20% FOR LIFE)

Make-Merch.com
Pre-loaded with templates, filters, & artwork, Make-Merch makes making Merch By Amazon designs simple and easy

MerchDesigner.com/editor
FREE web-based designer for Merch By Amazon designs

DesignPickle.com
UNLIMITED graphic design requests for one monthly fee! Visit **MerchPickle.com** and use code CG2017 to save 30%!

Join the Facebook Group:
Facebook.com/groups/MerchLife
OR **www.merch.group**

Learn about Merch By Amazon with the Merch Life book:
Amazon.com/dp/1517795990

Merch By Amazon Udemy Courses
Udemy.com/merchbyamazonintro – Introduction
Udemy.com/merchbyamazon - Advanced

I hope that you find this sketchbook for Merch By Amazon useful!
Please let me know if I can help you in any way.

Message me through Facebook at:
facebook.com/chris
Or use this link: **m.me/chris**

Please also visit **ChrisGreen.com**

Find all of my books at:
Amazon.com/author/chris

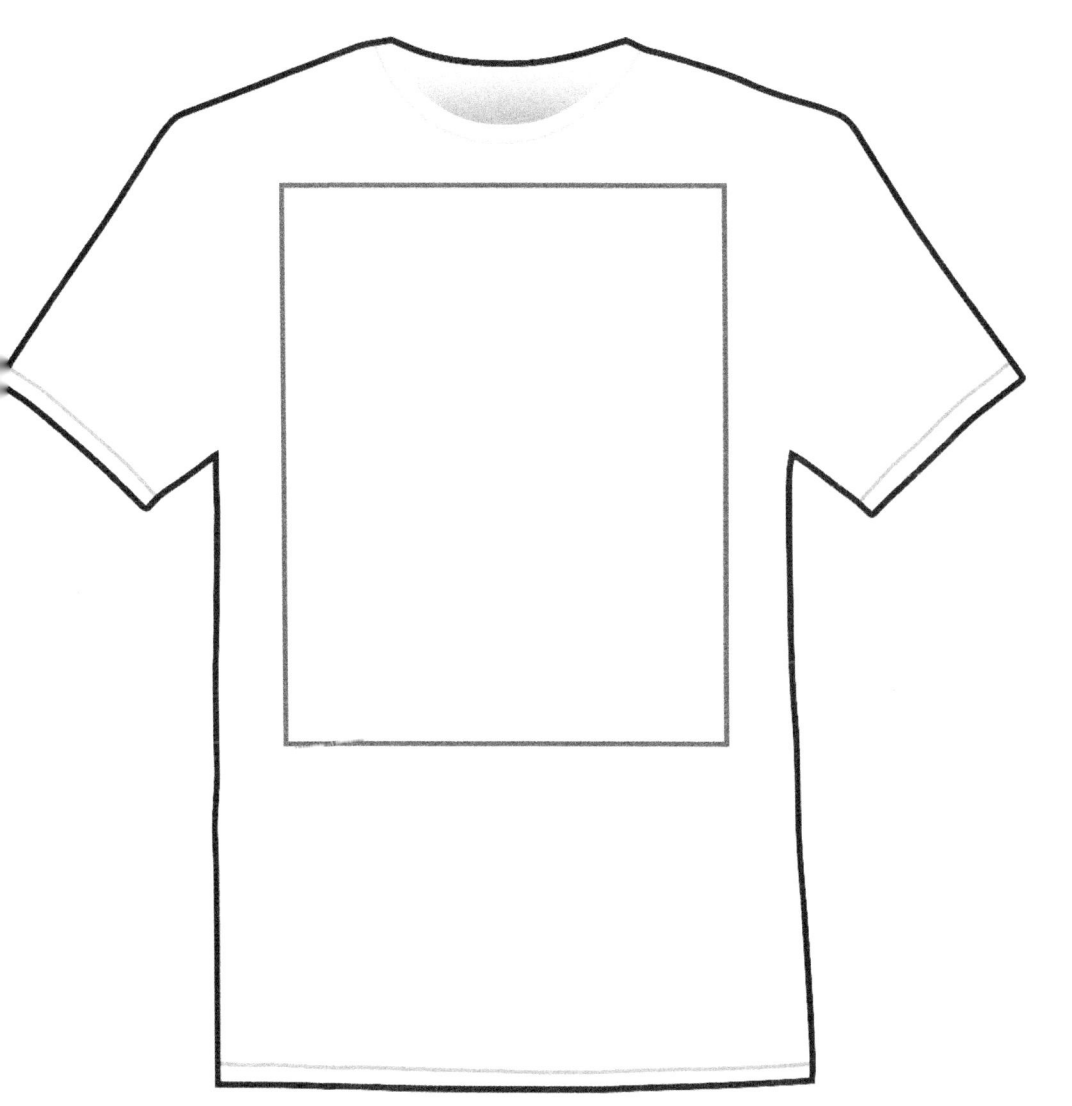

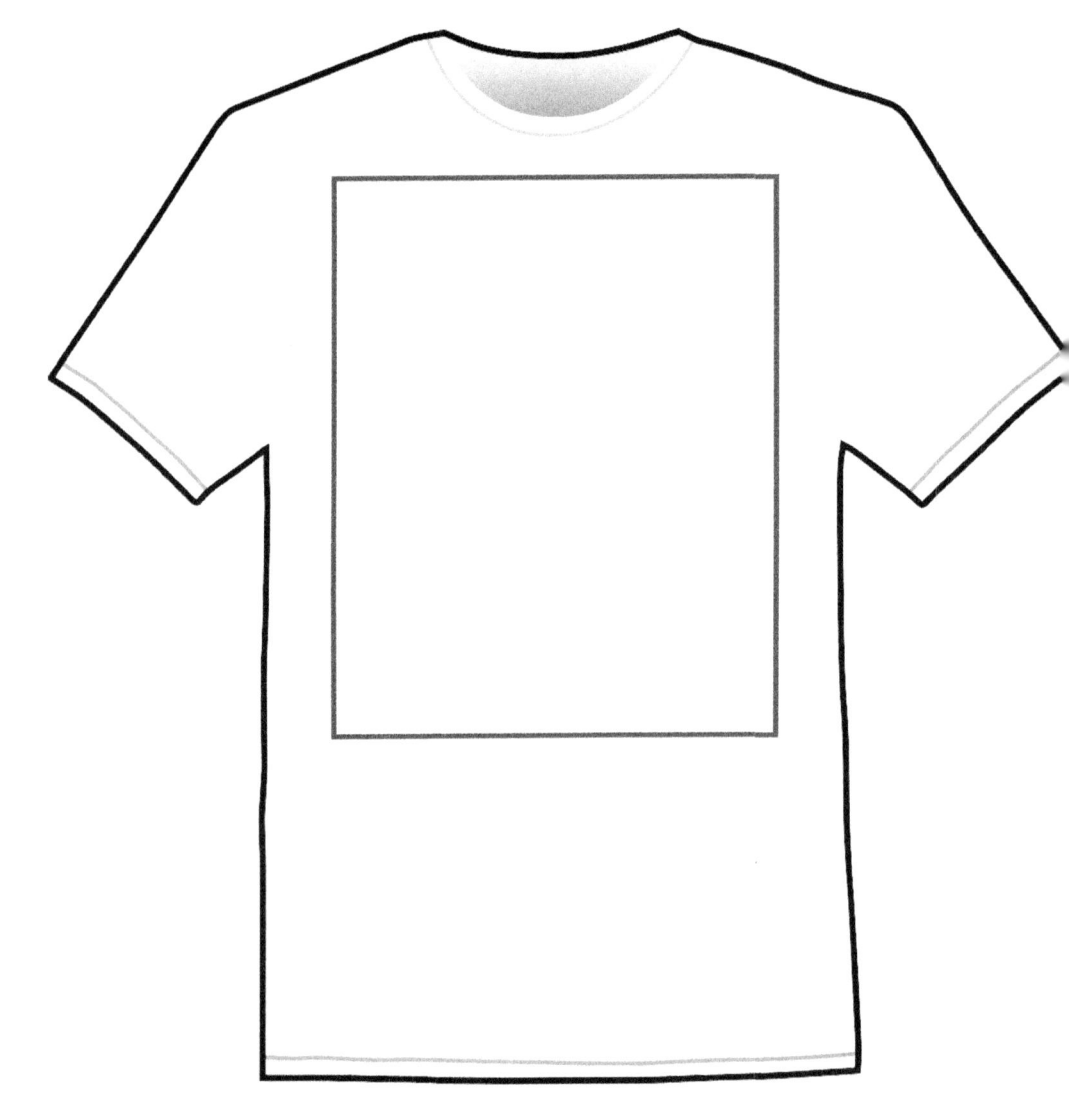

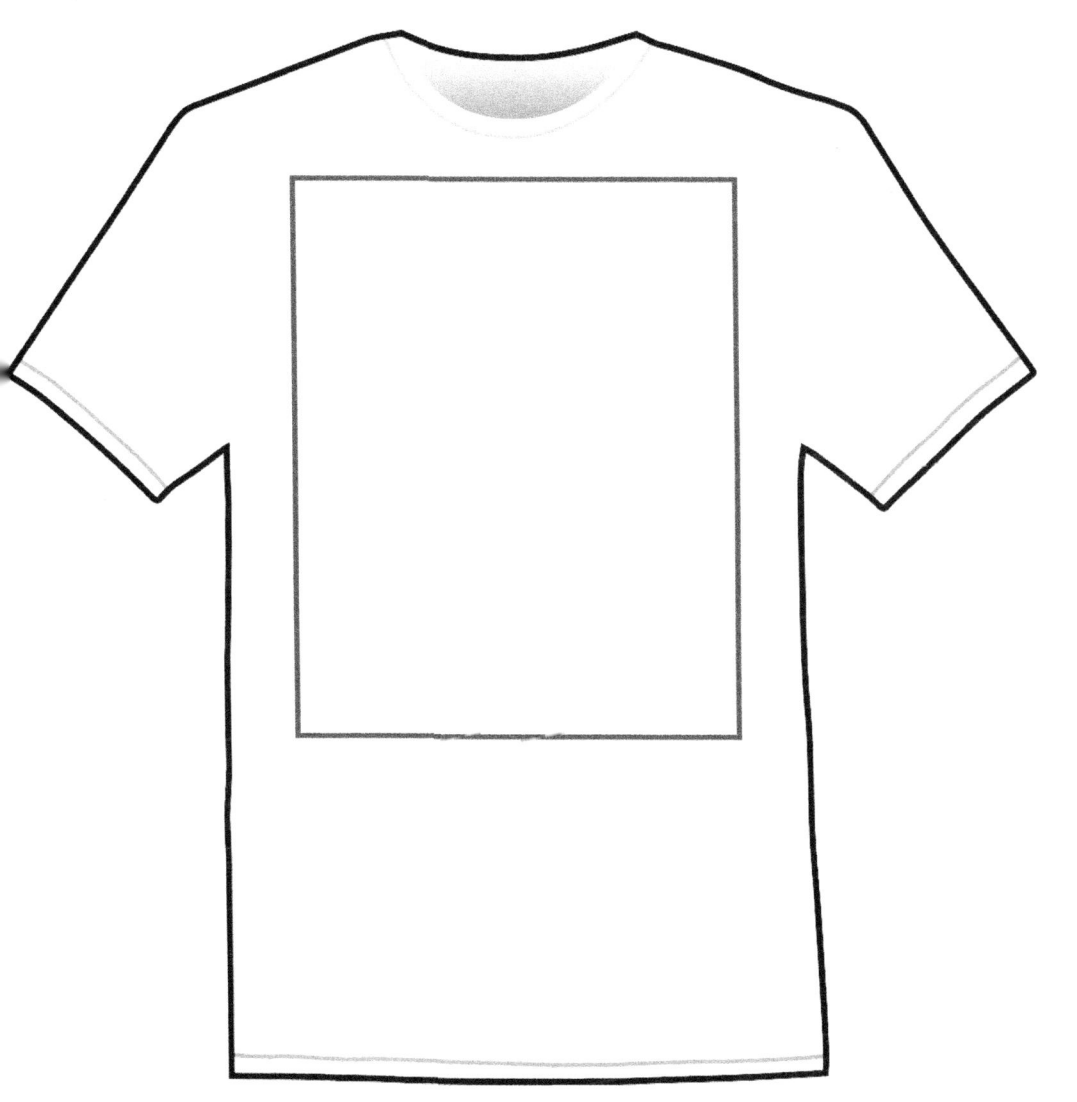

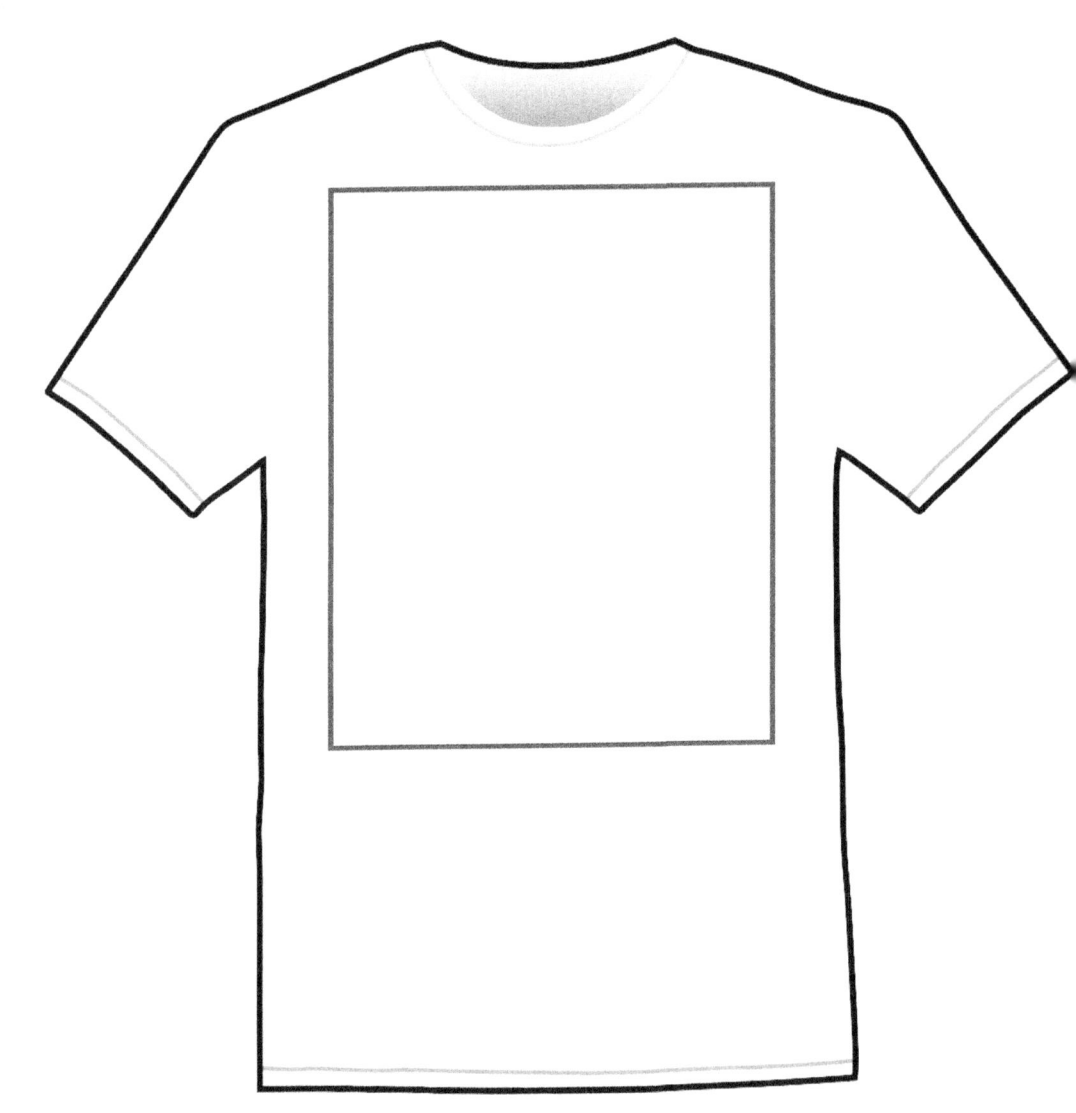

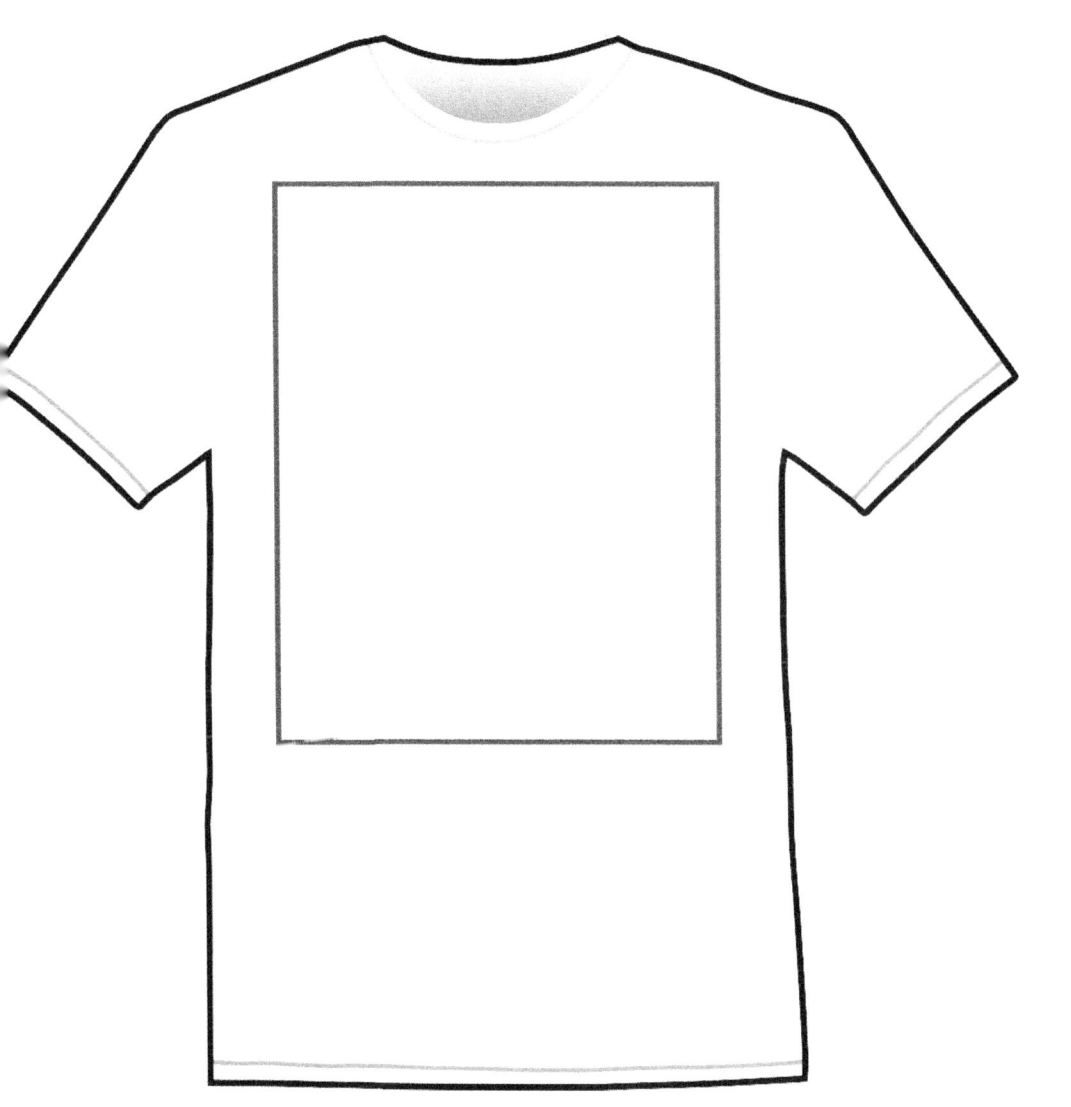

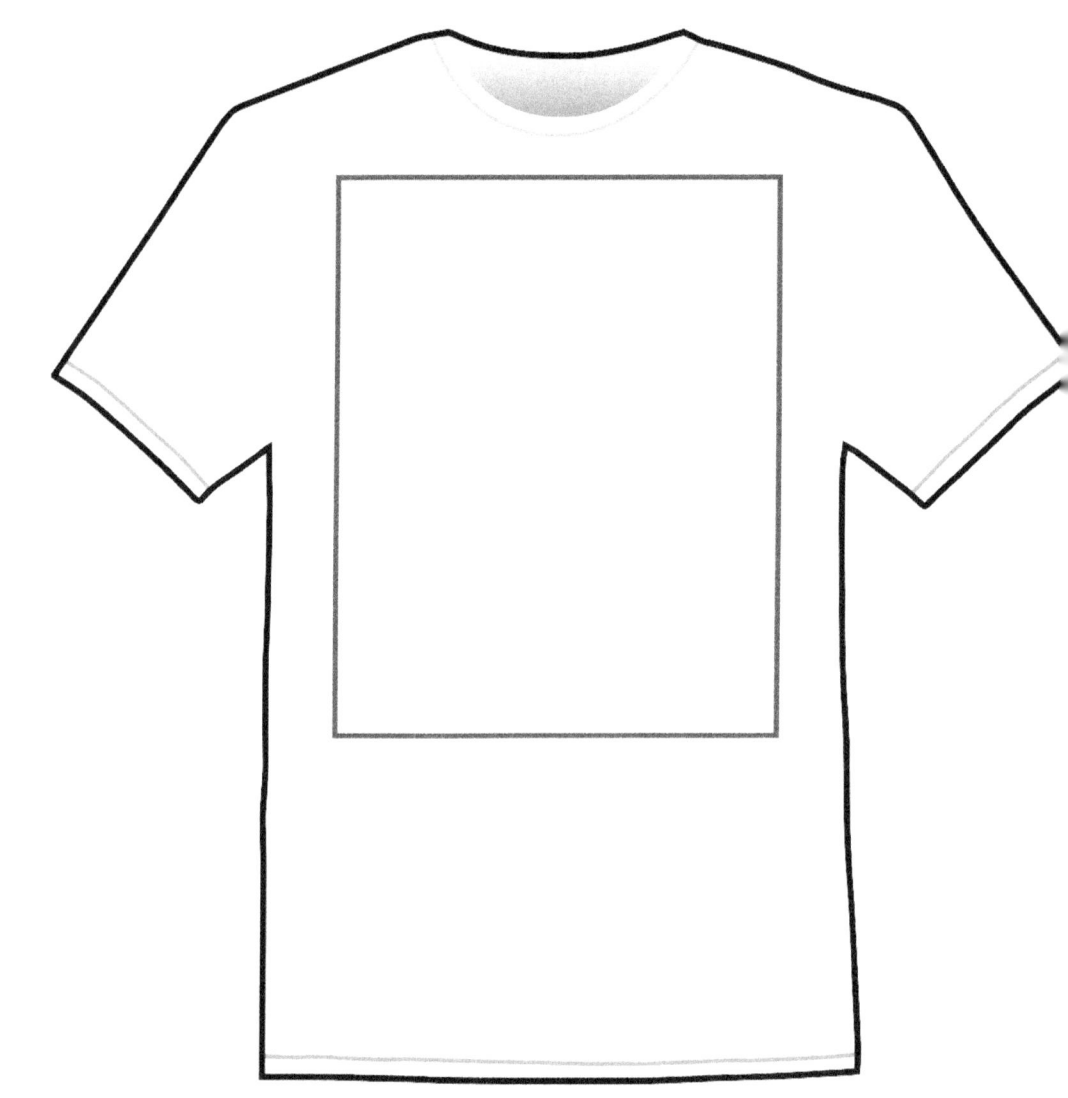

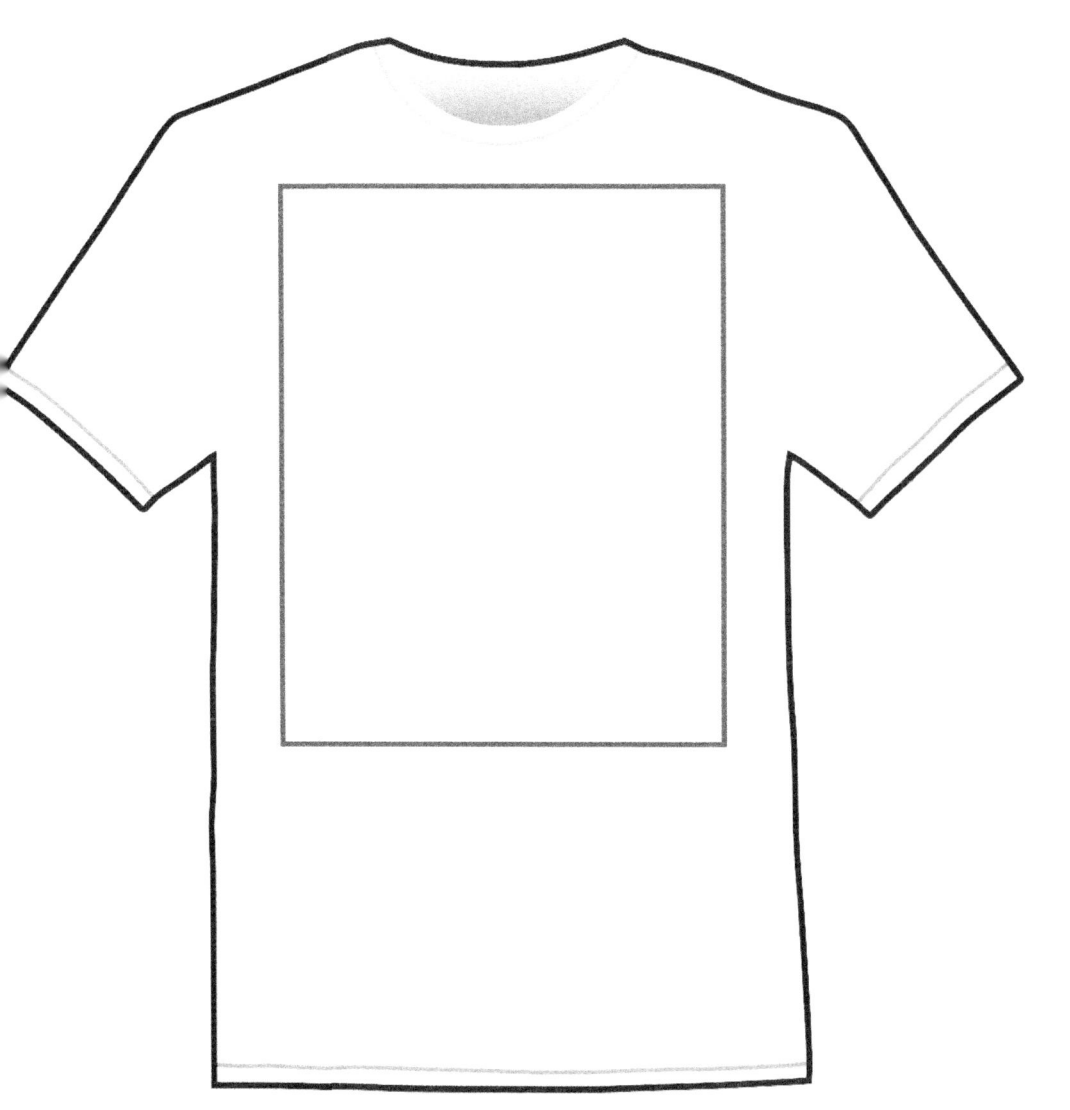

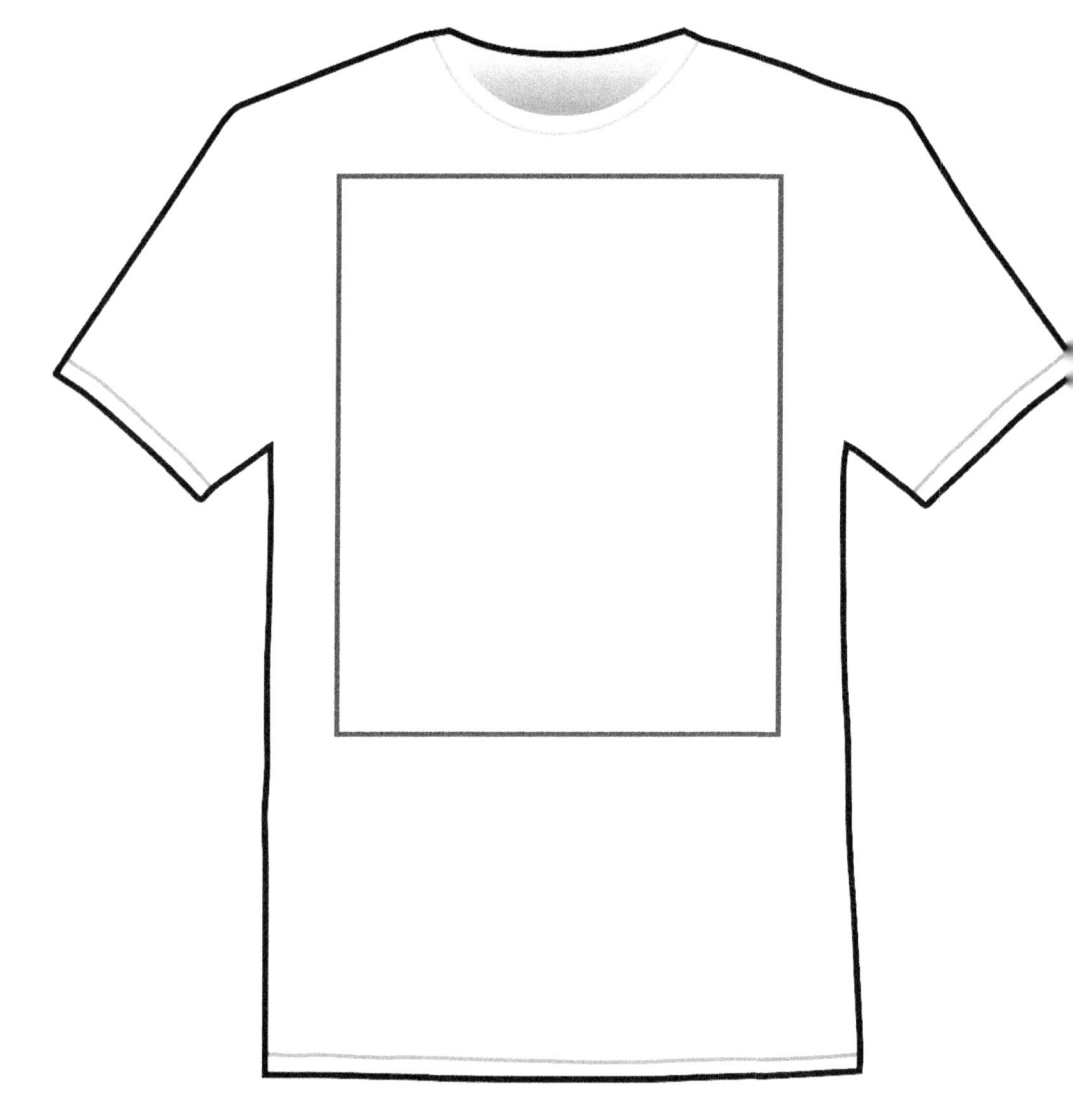

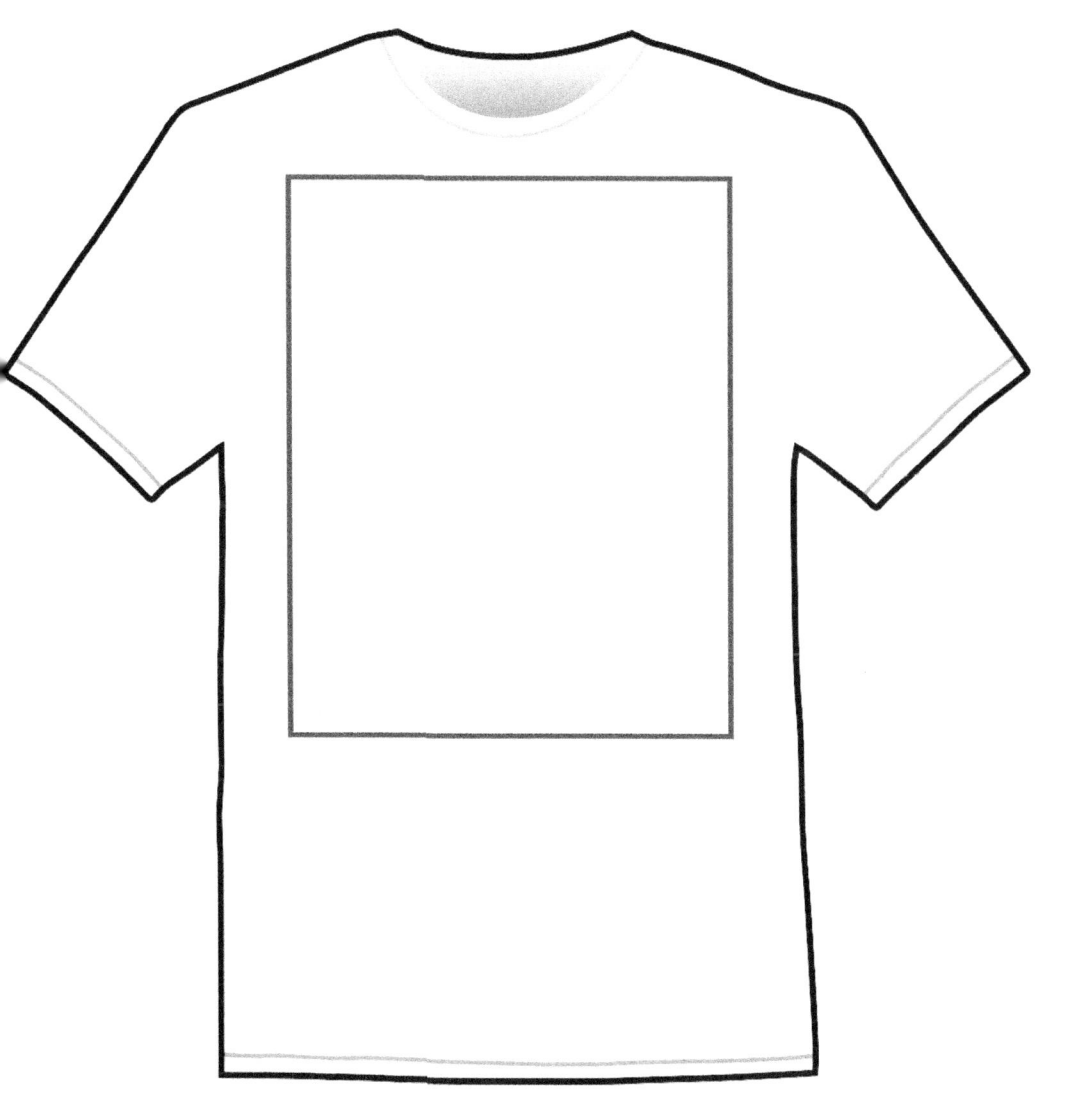

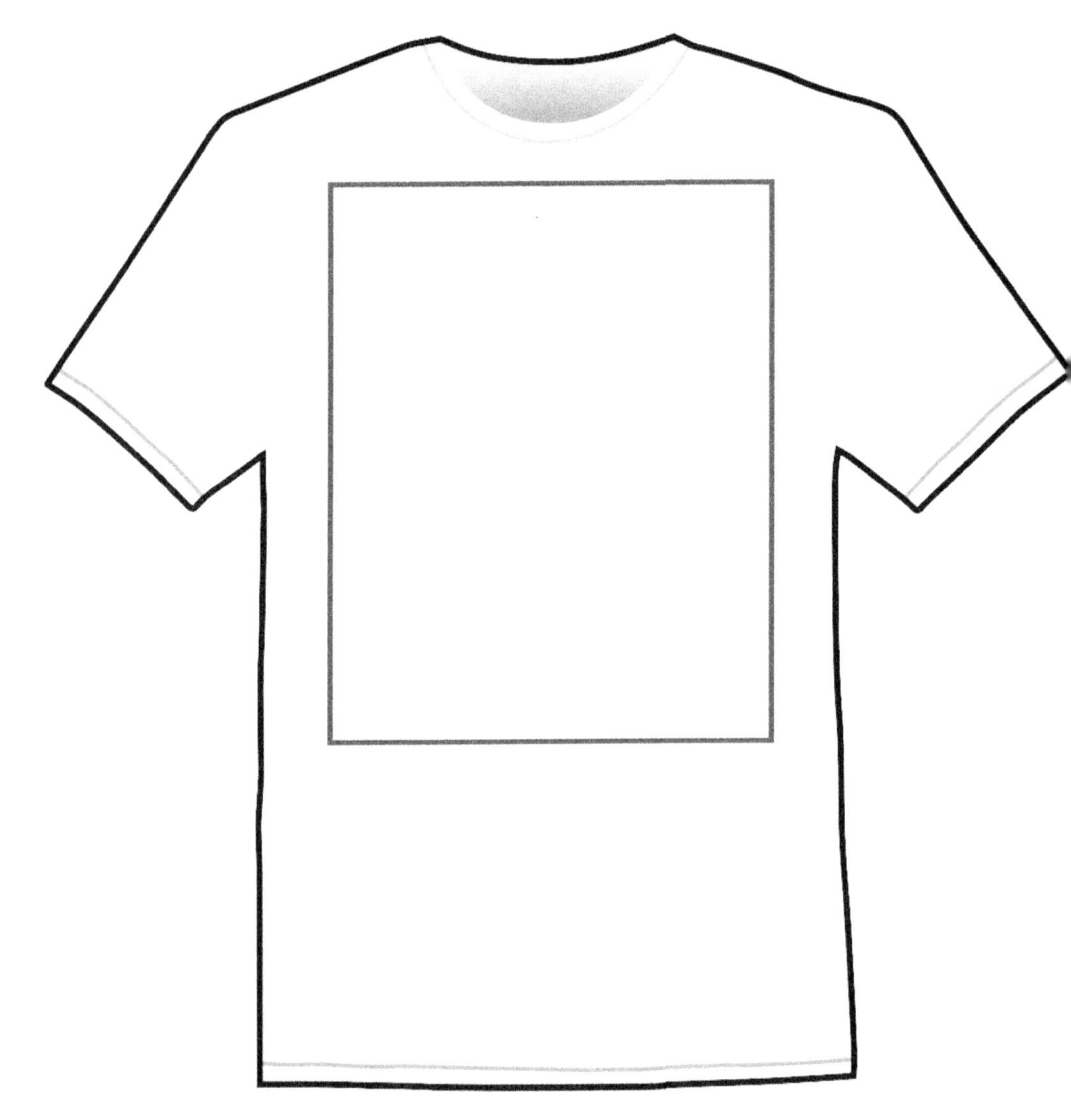

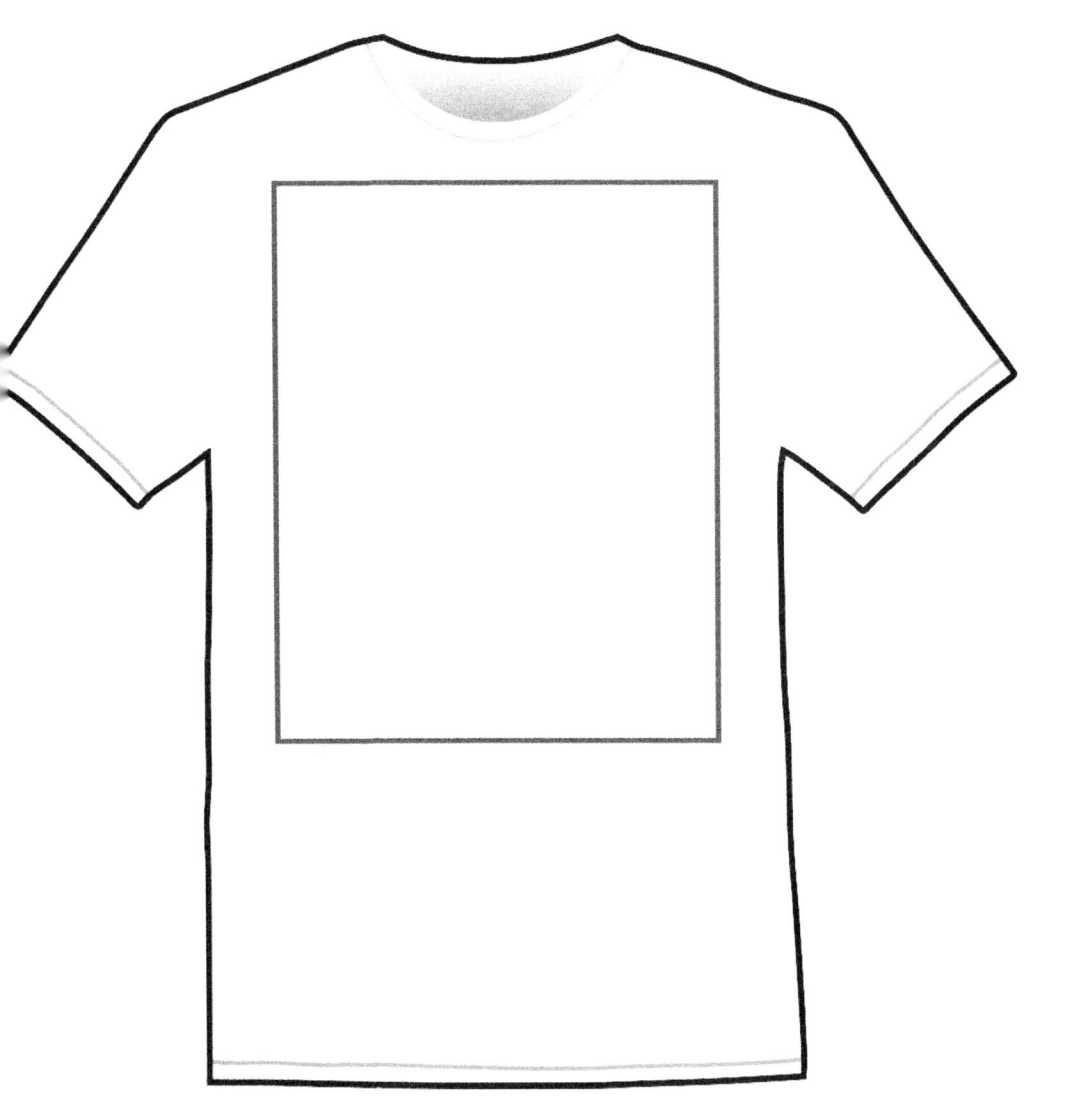

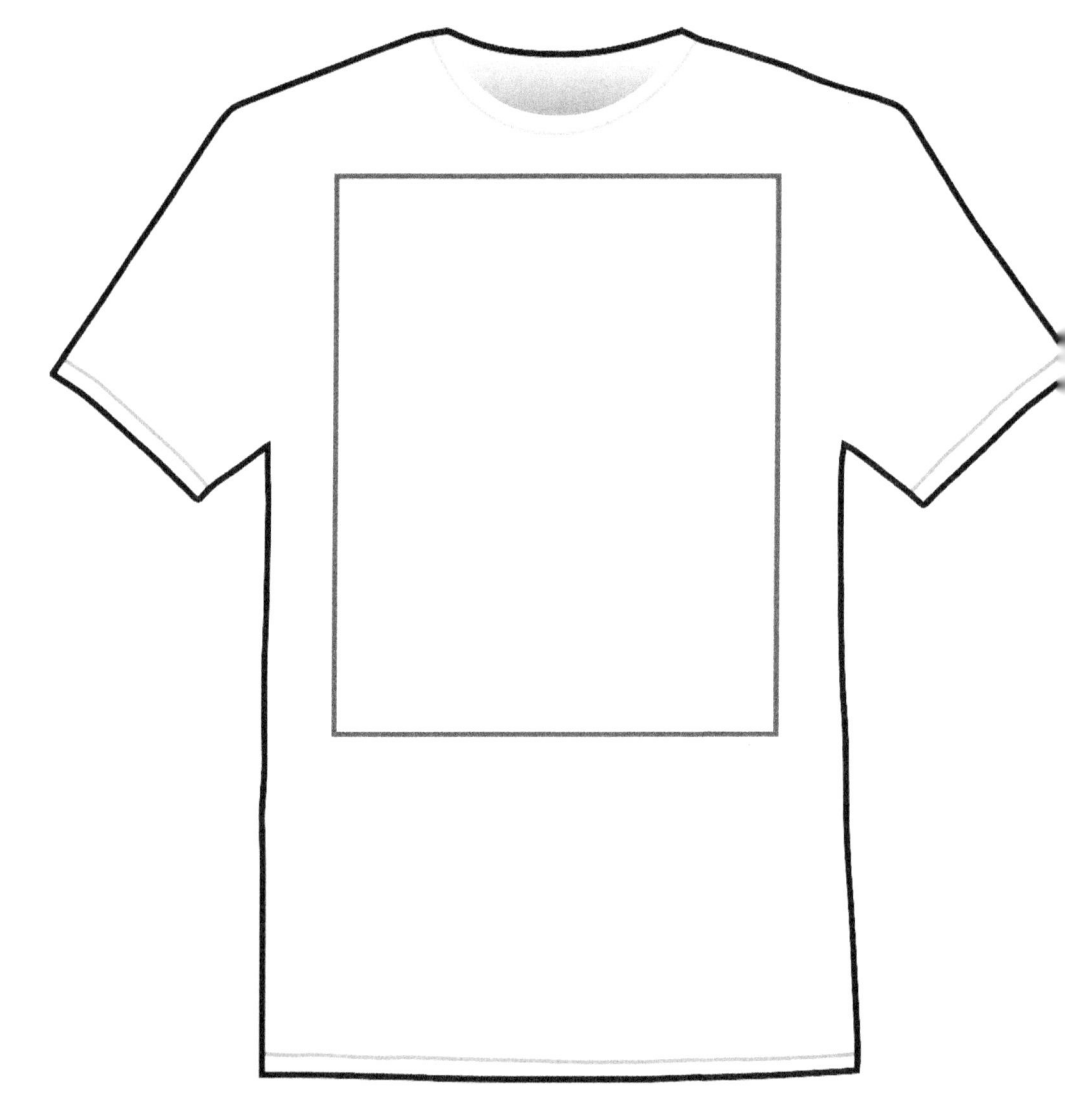

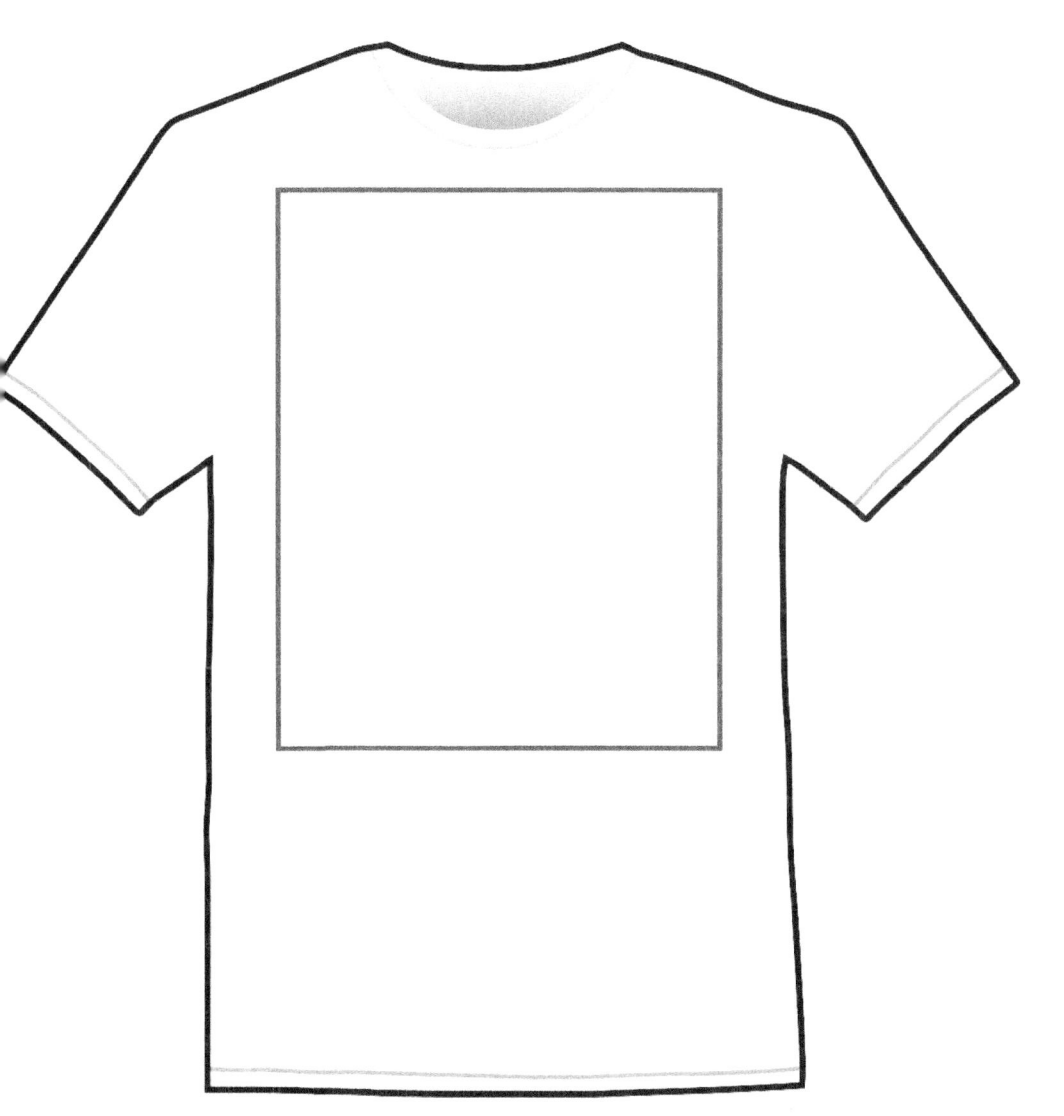

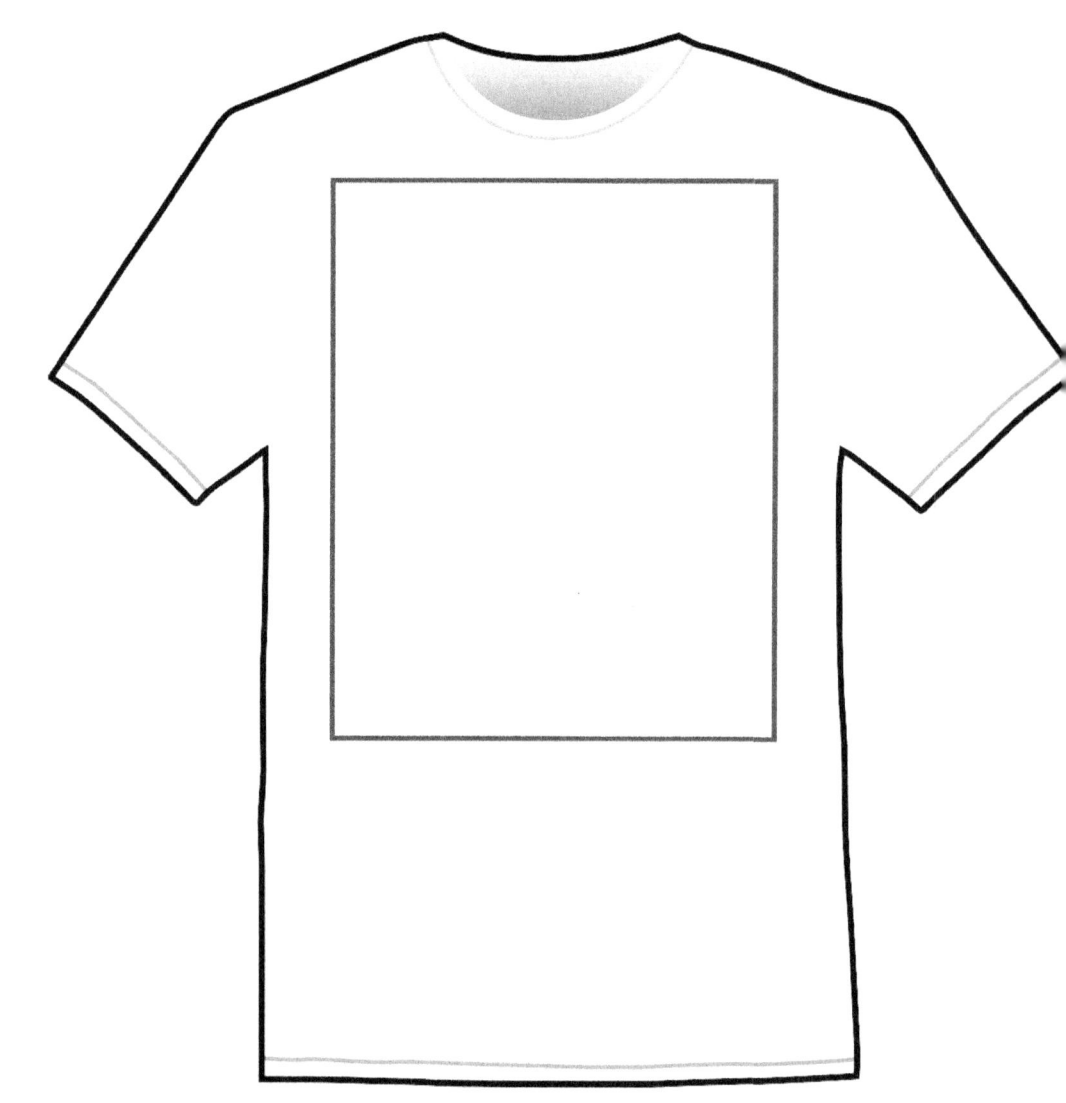

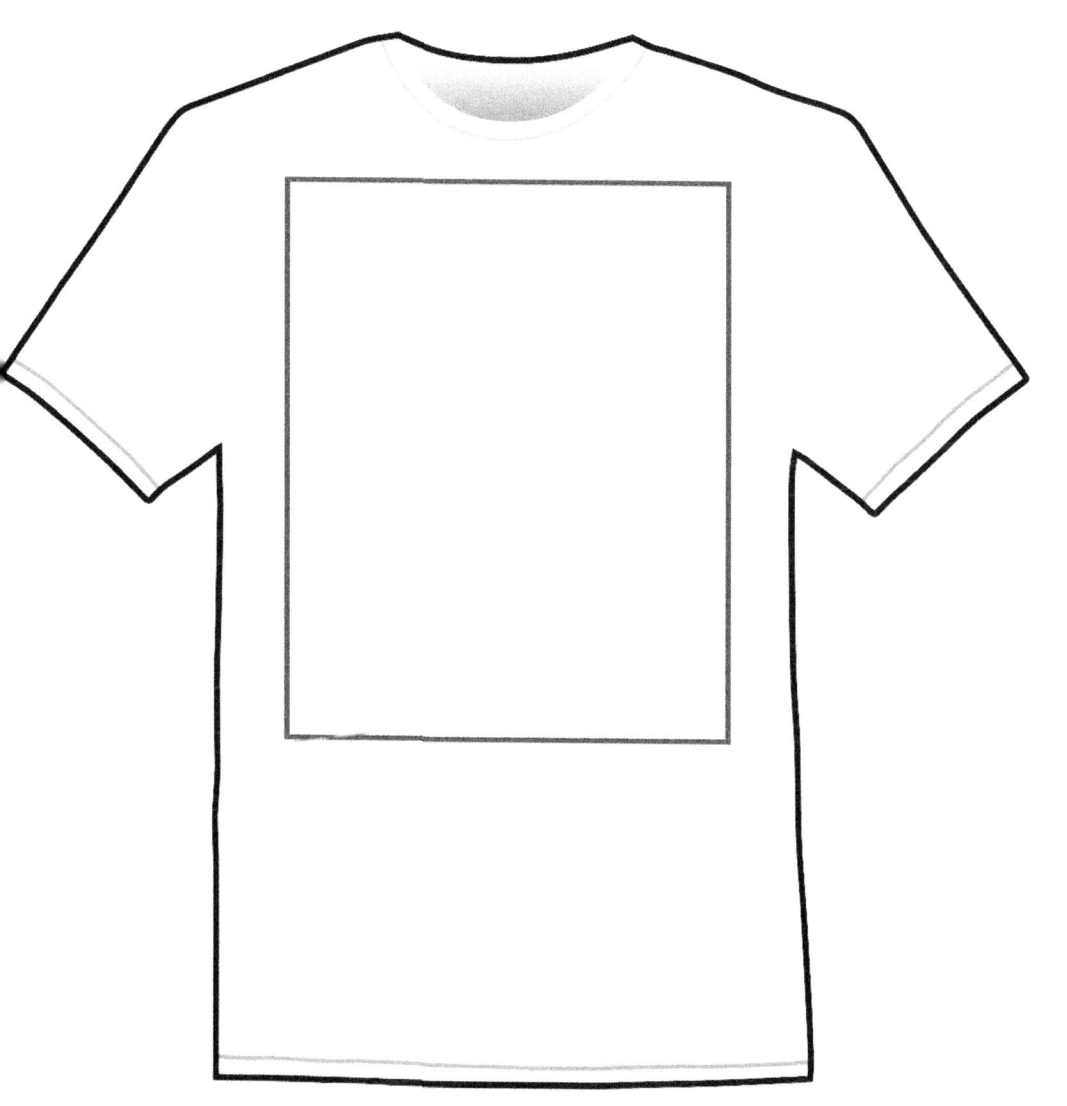

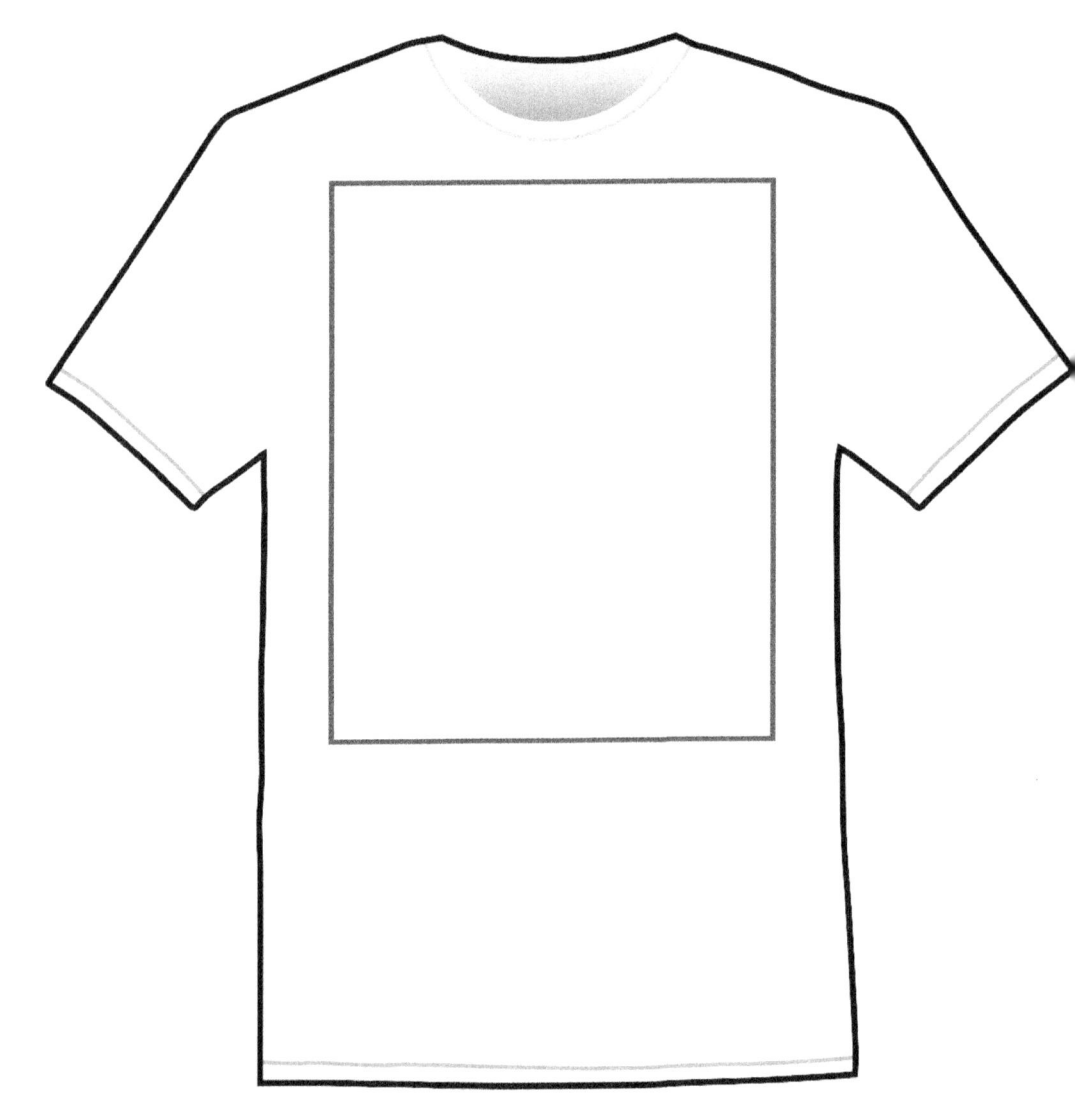

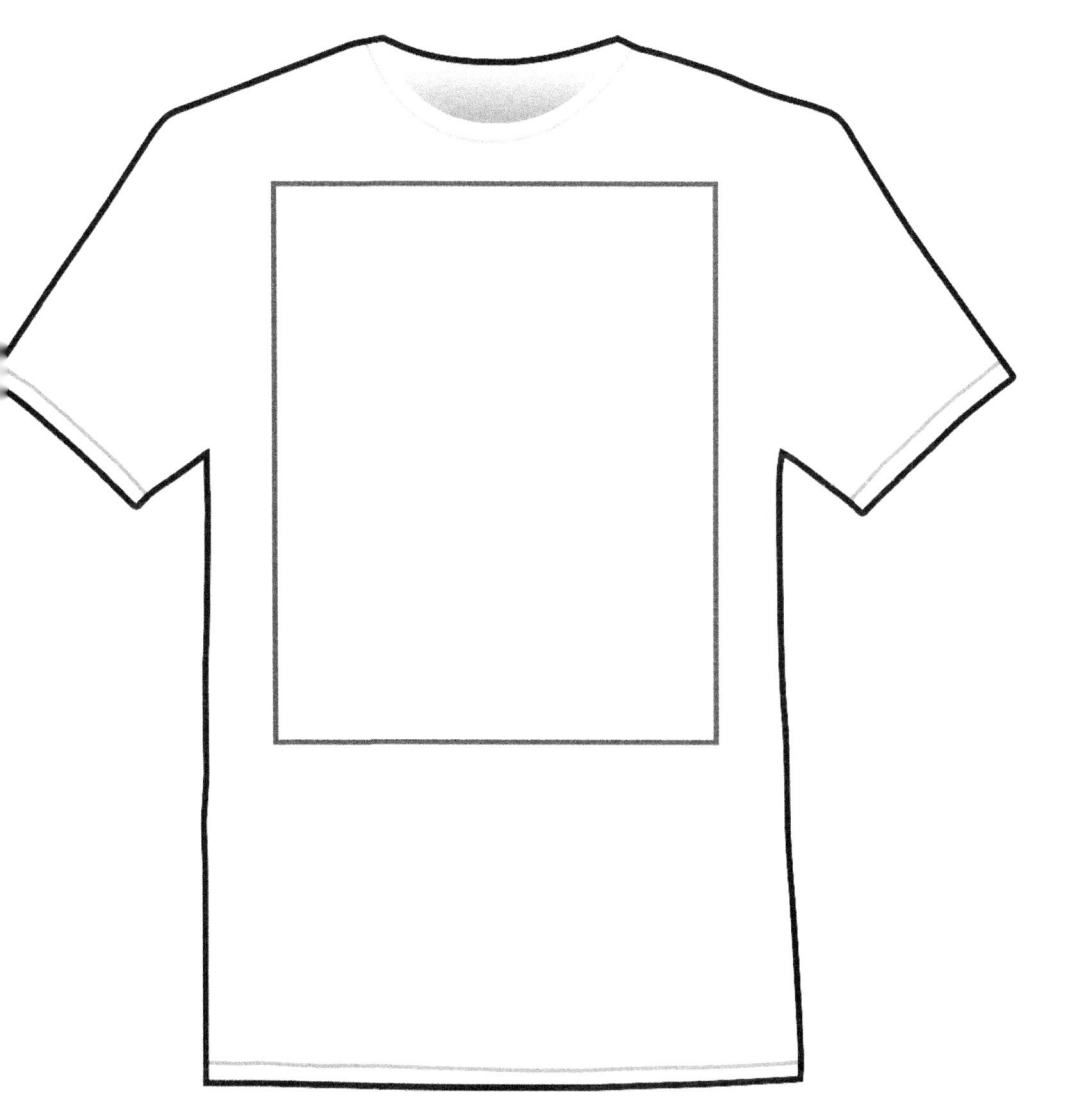

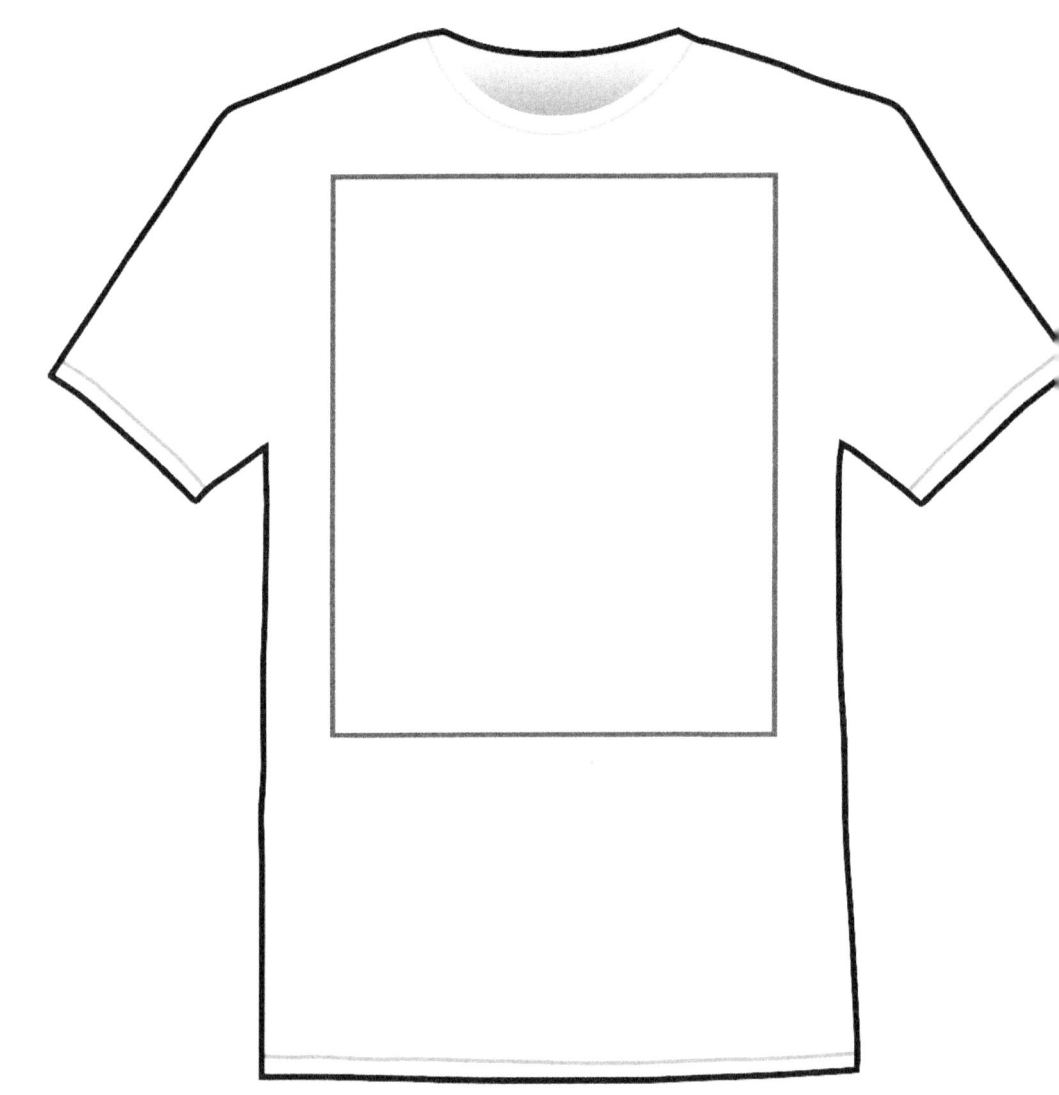

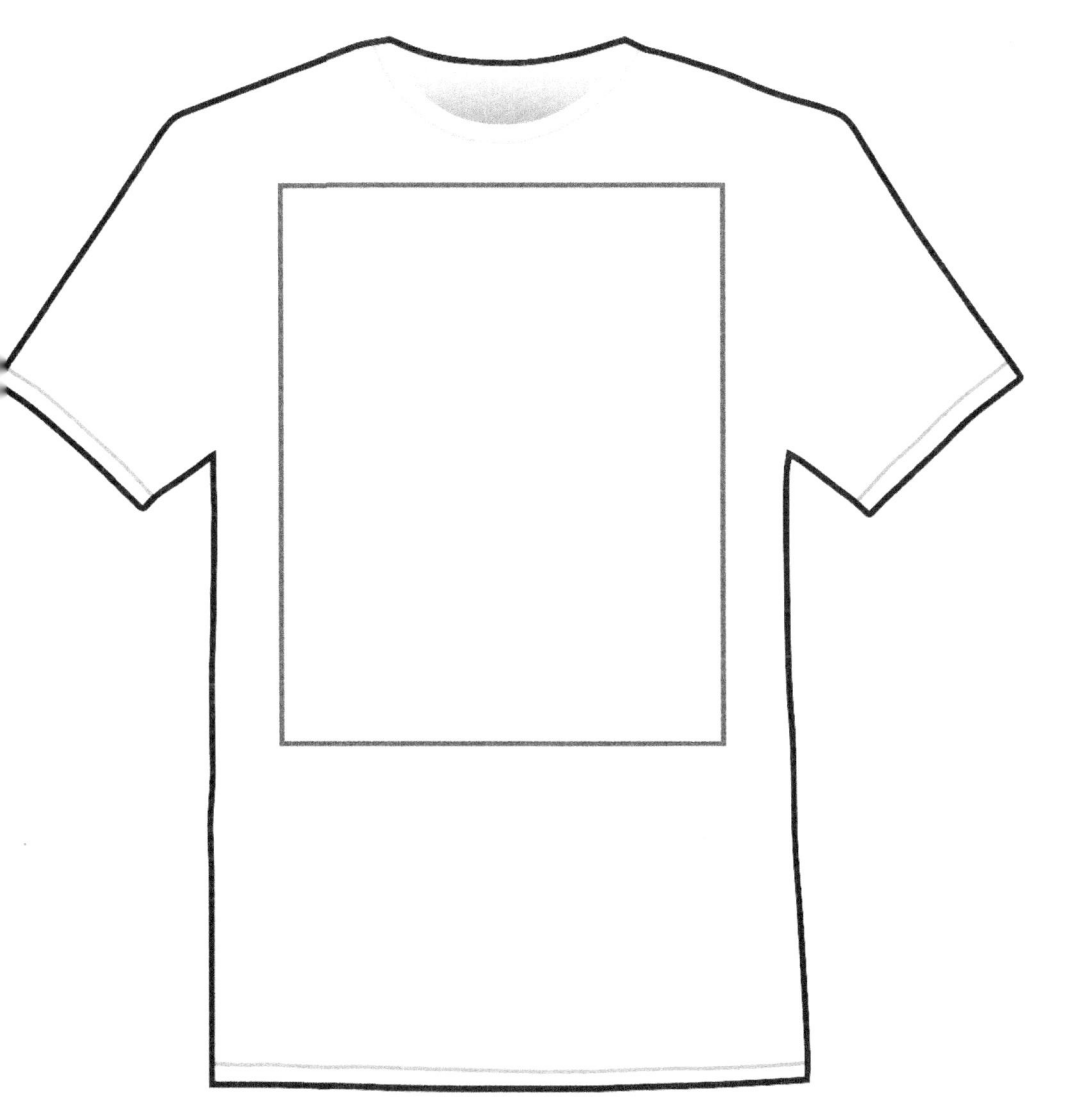

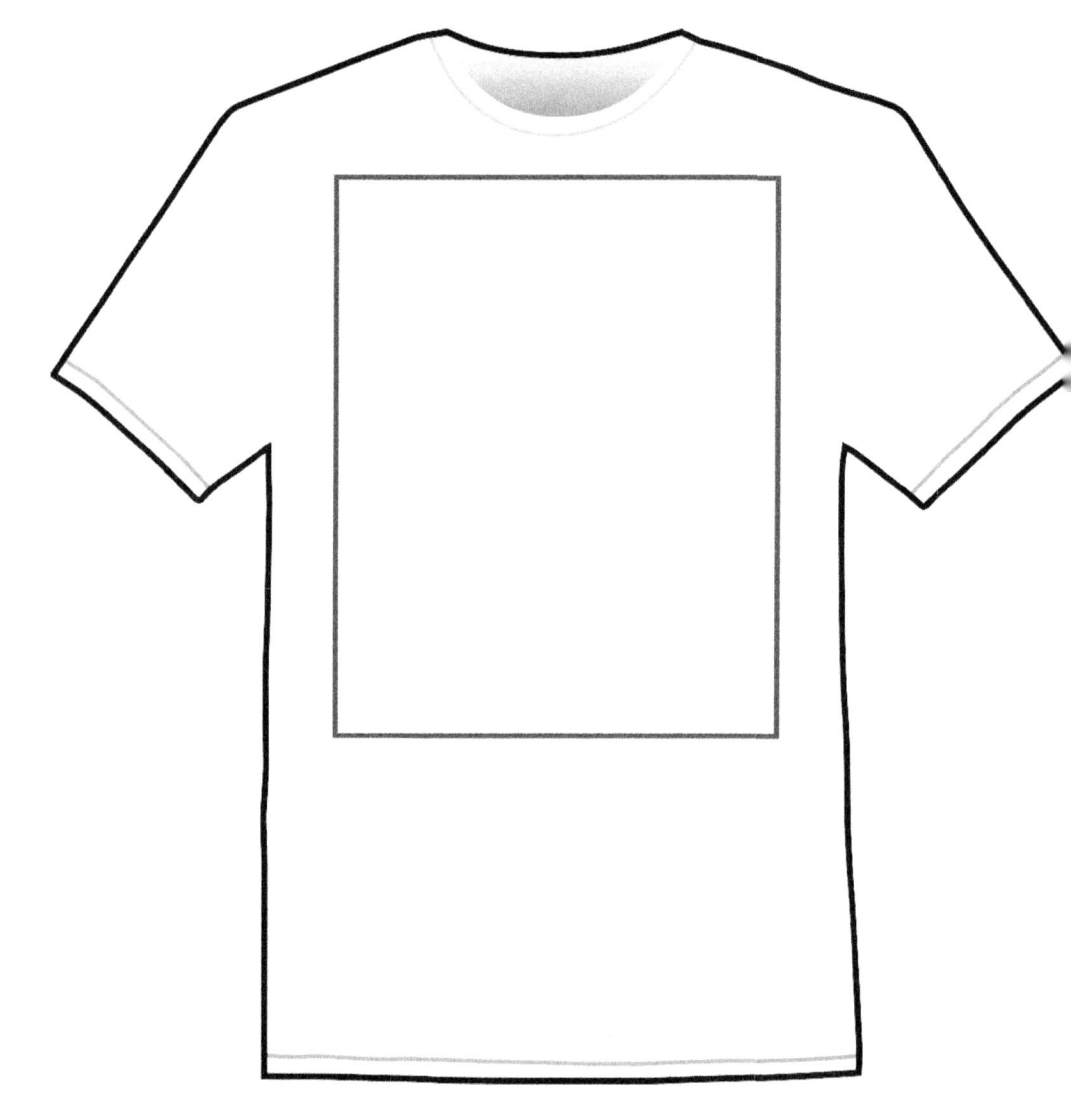

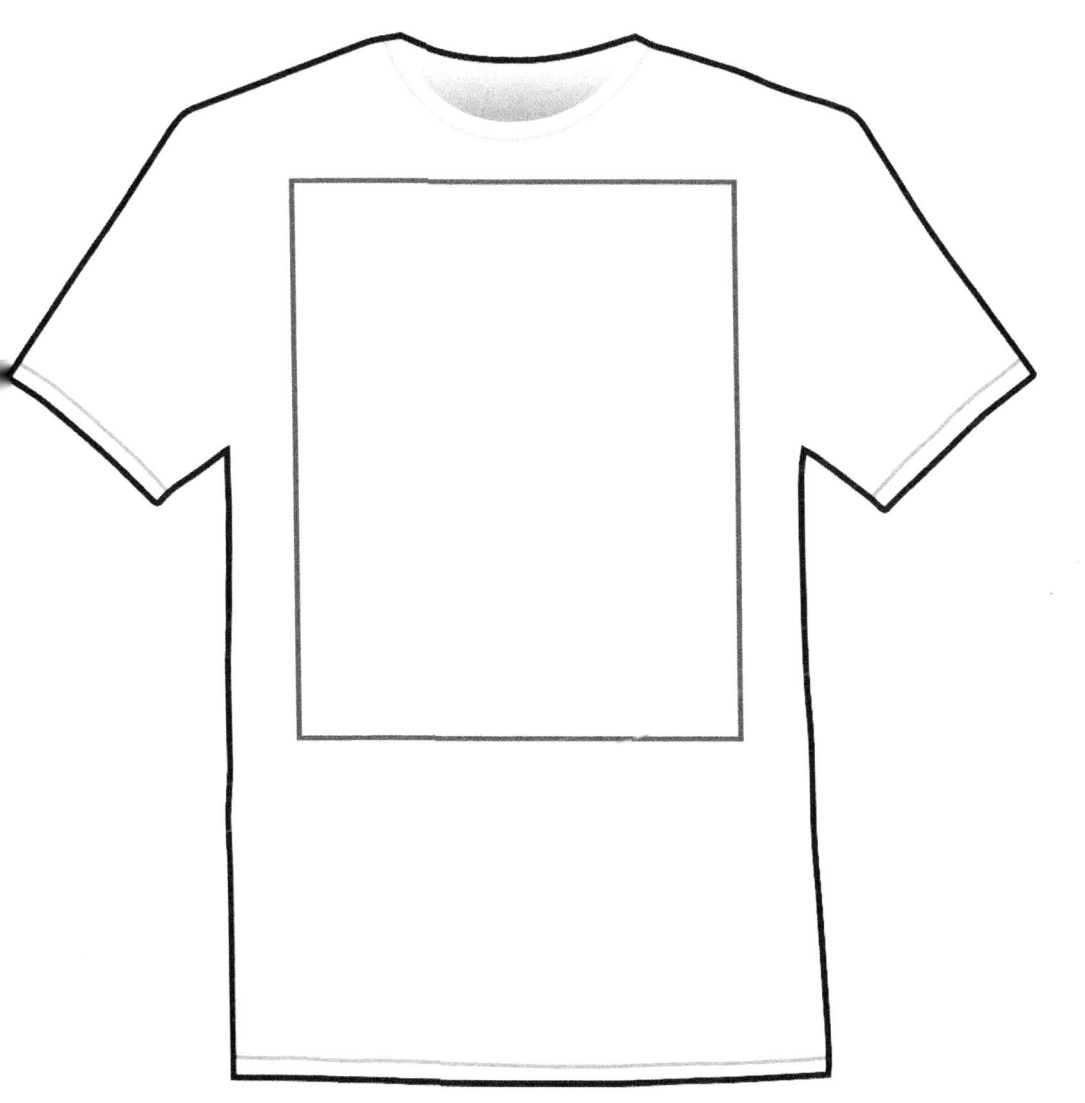

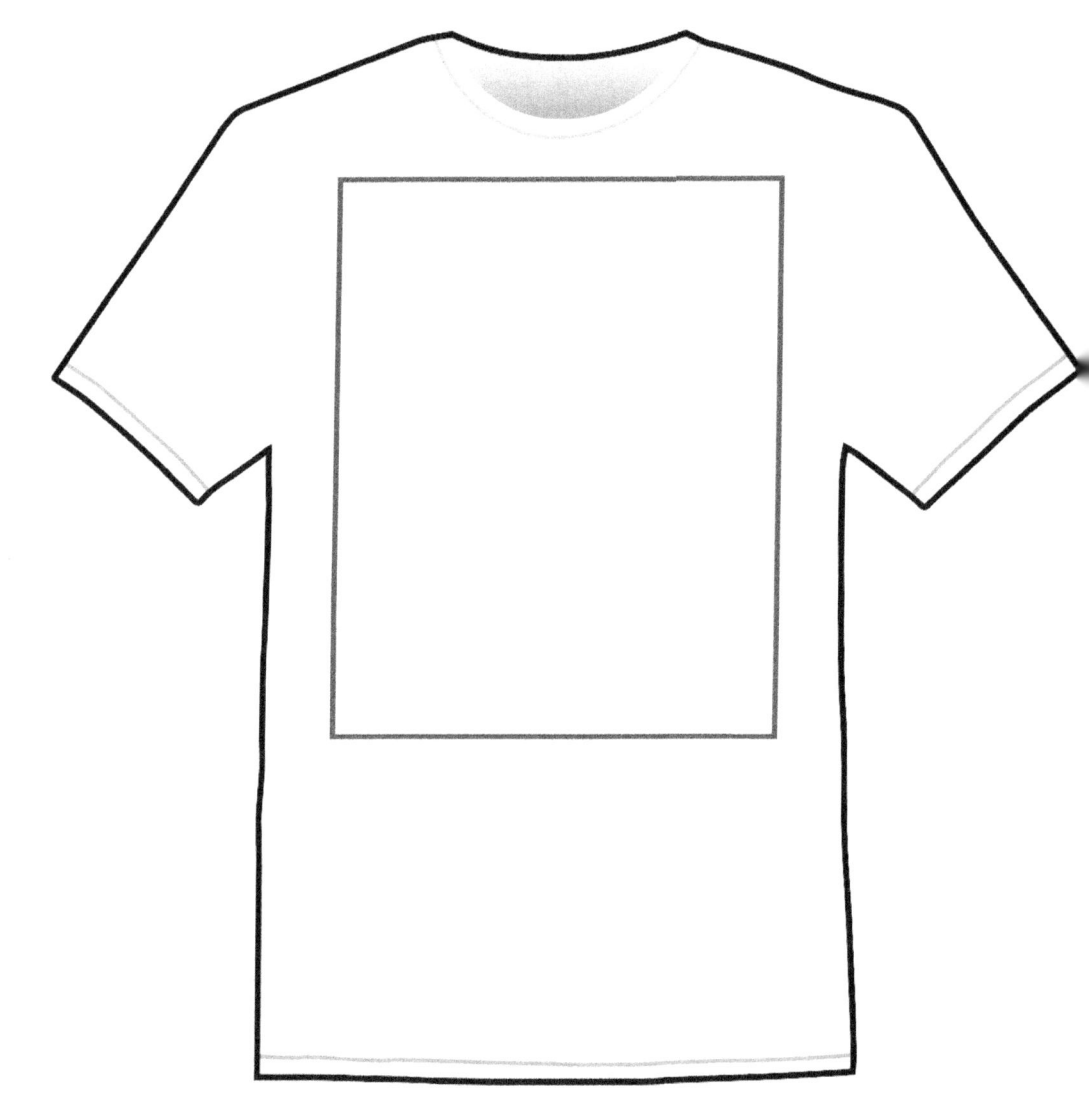

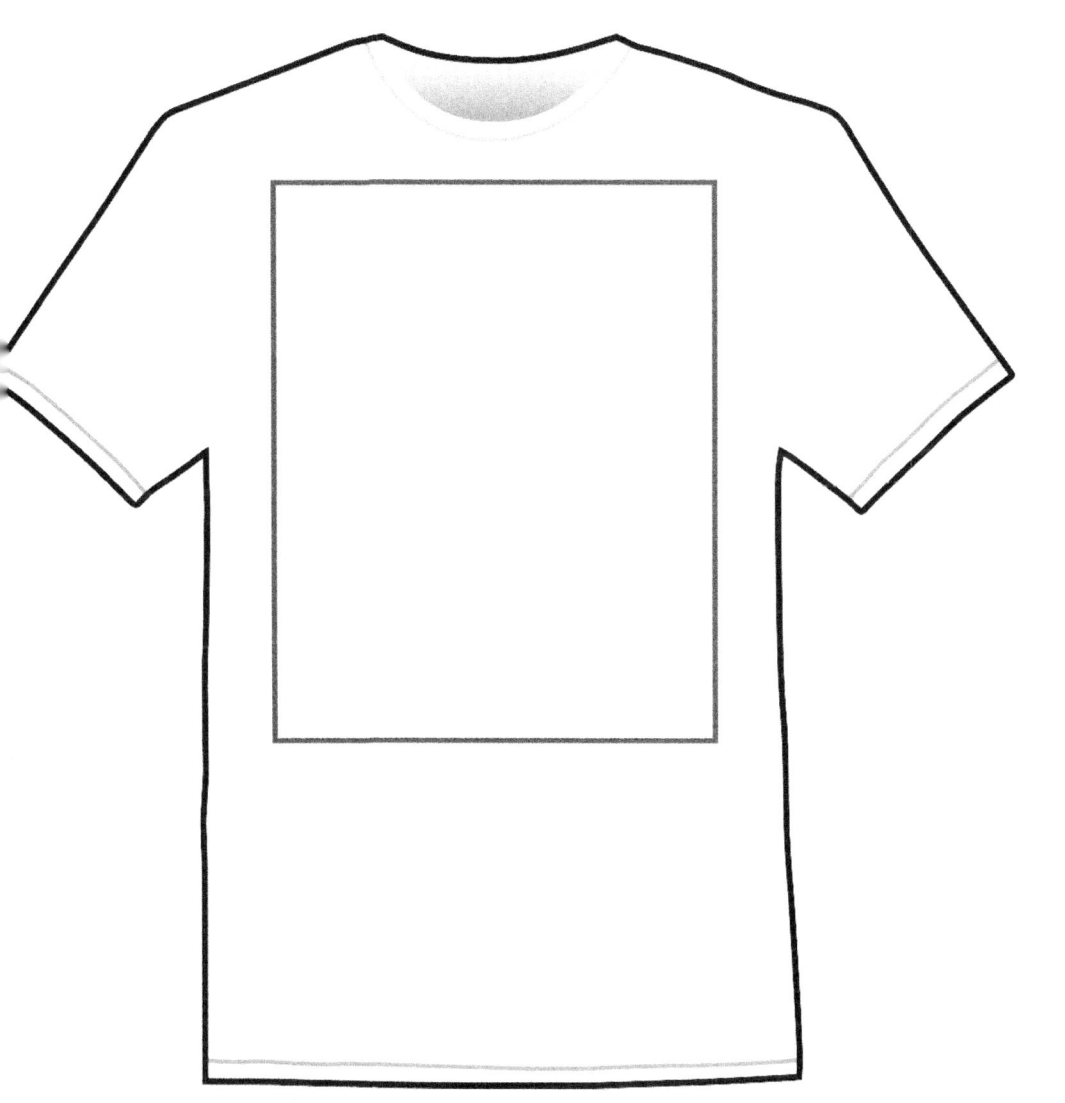

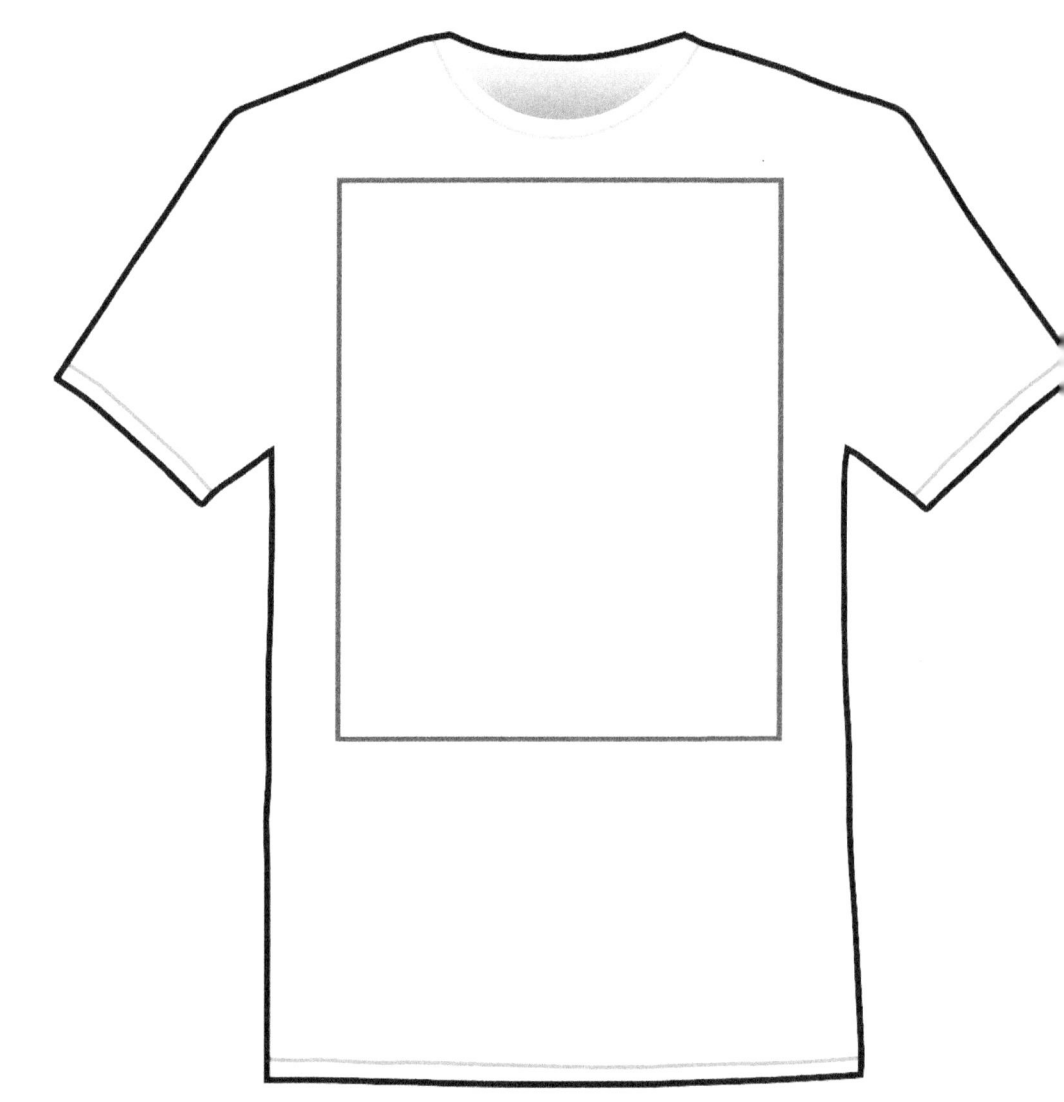

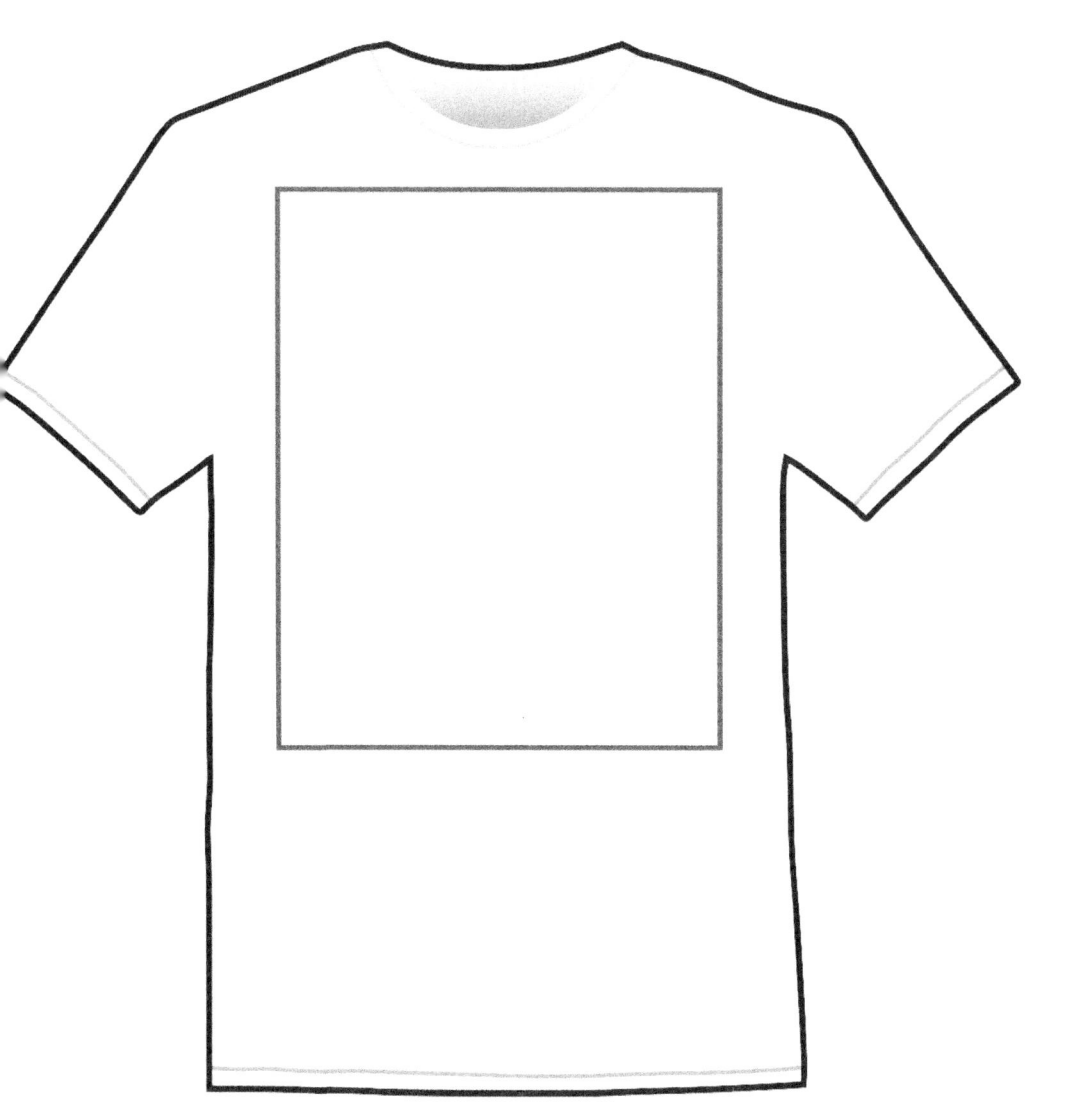

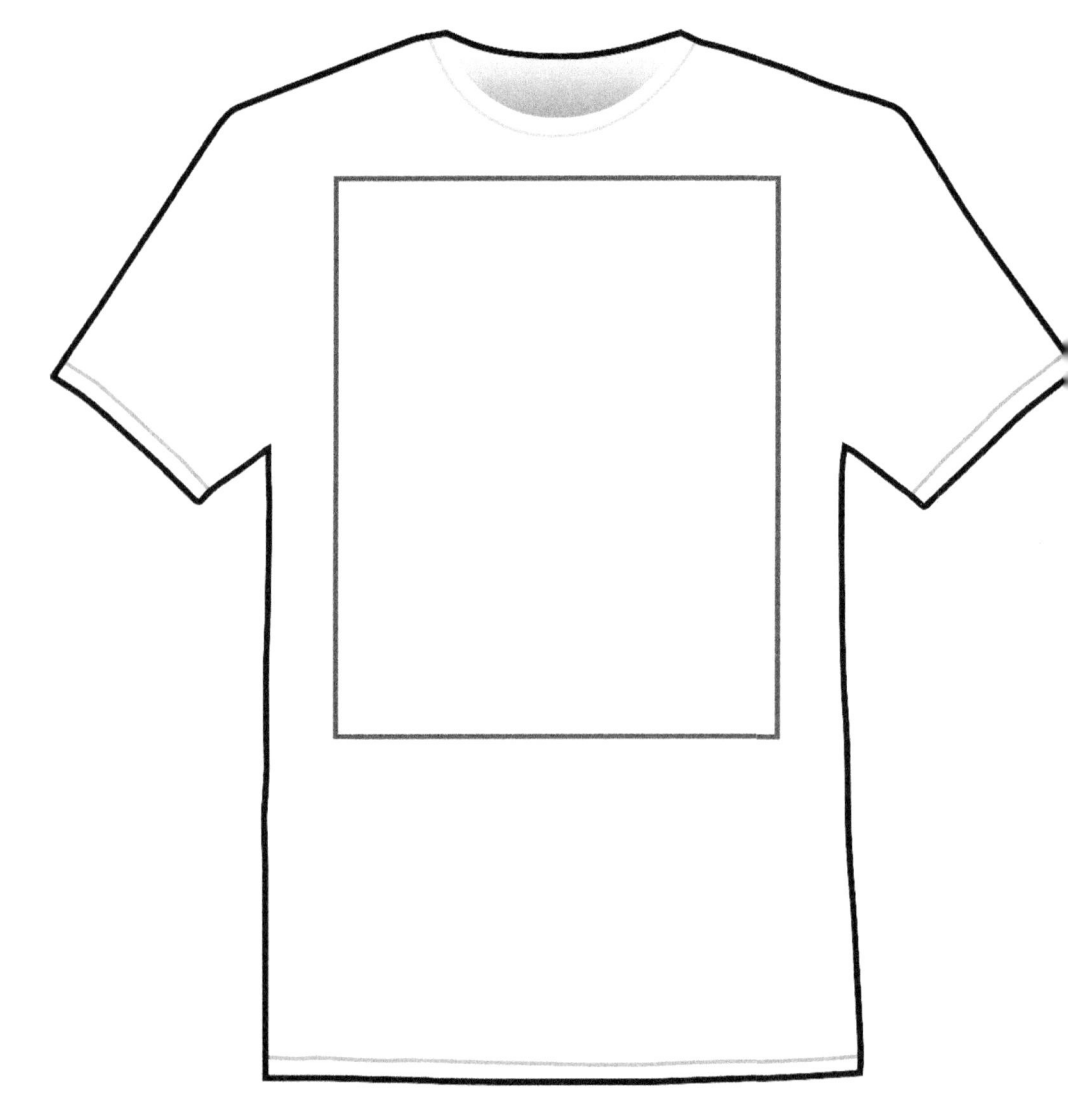

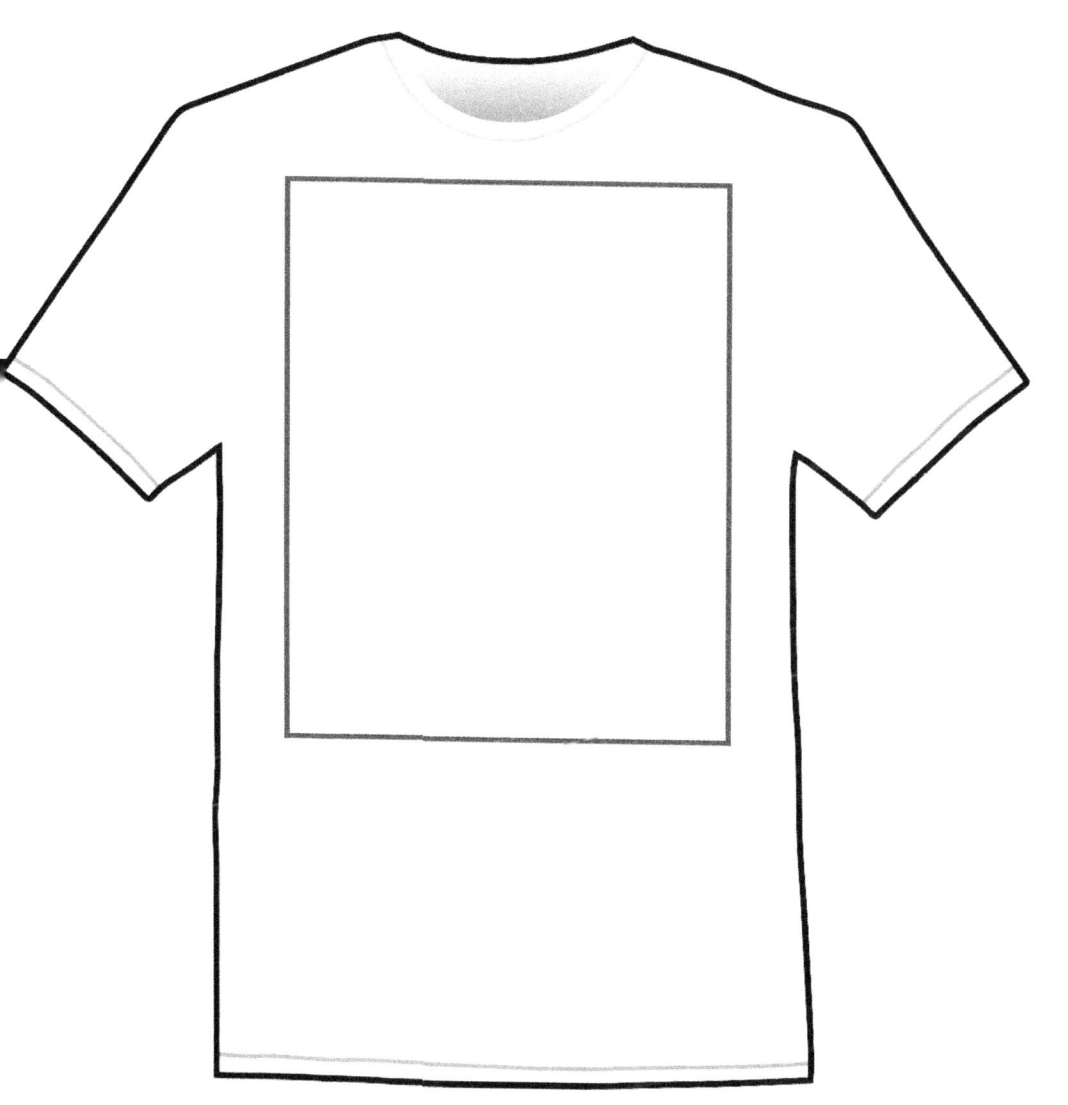

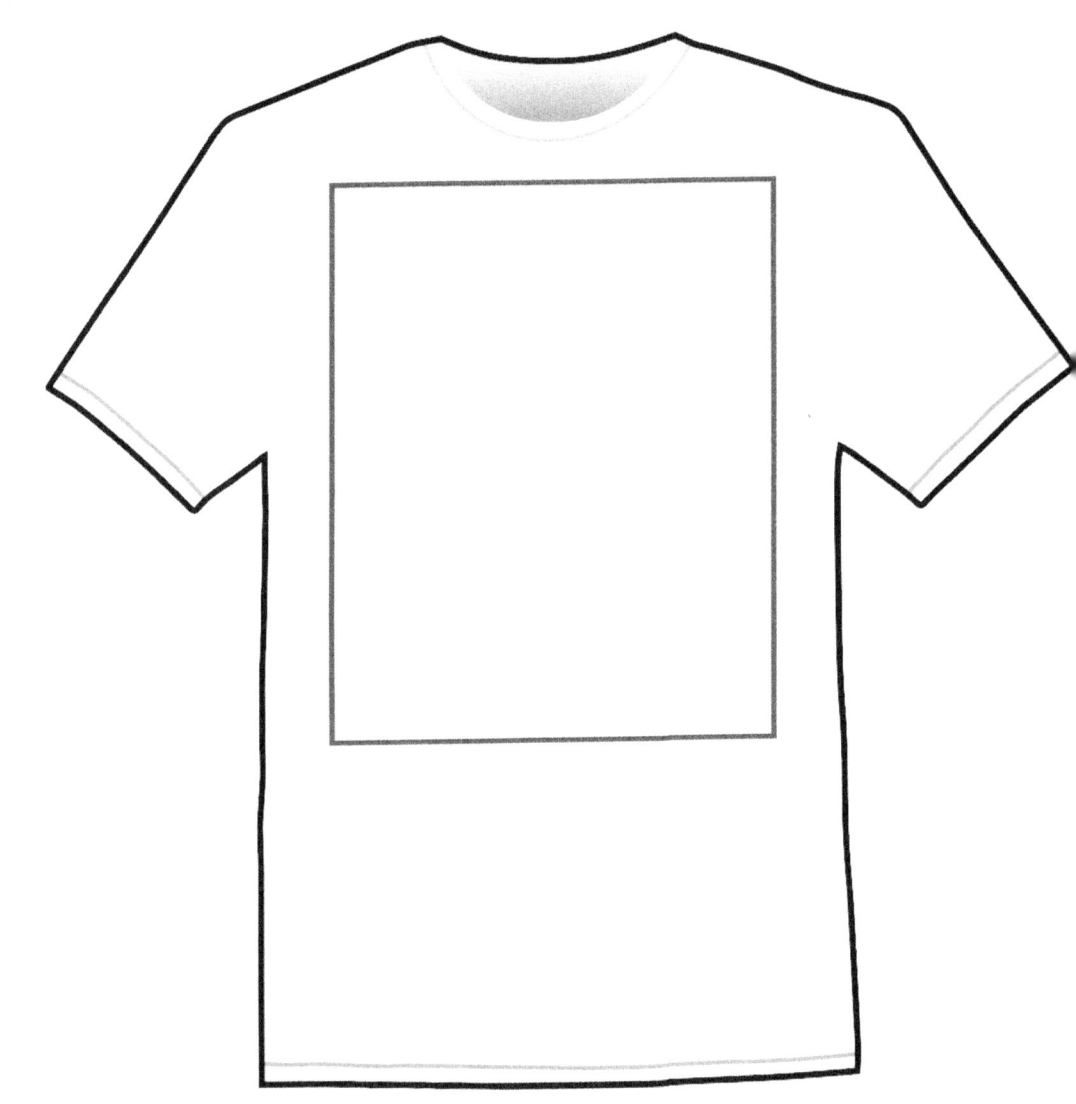

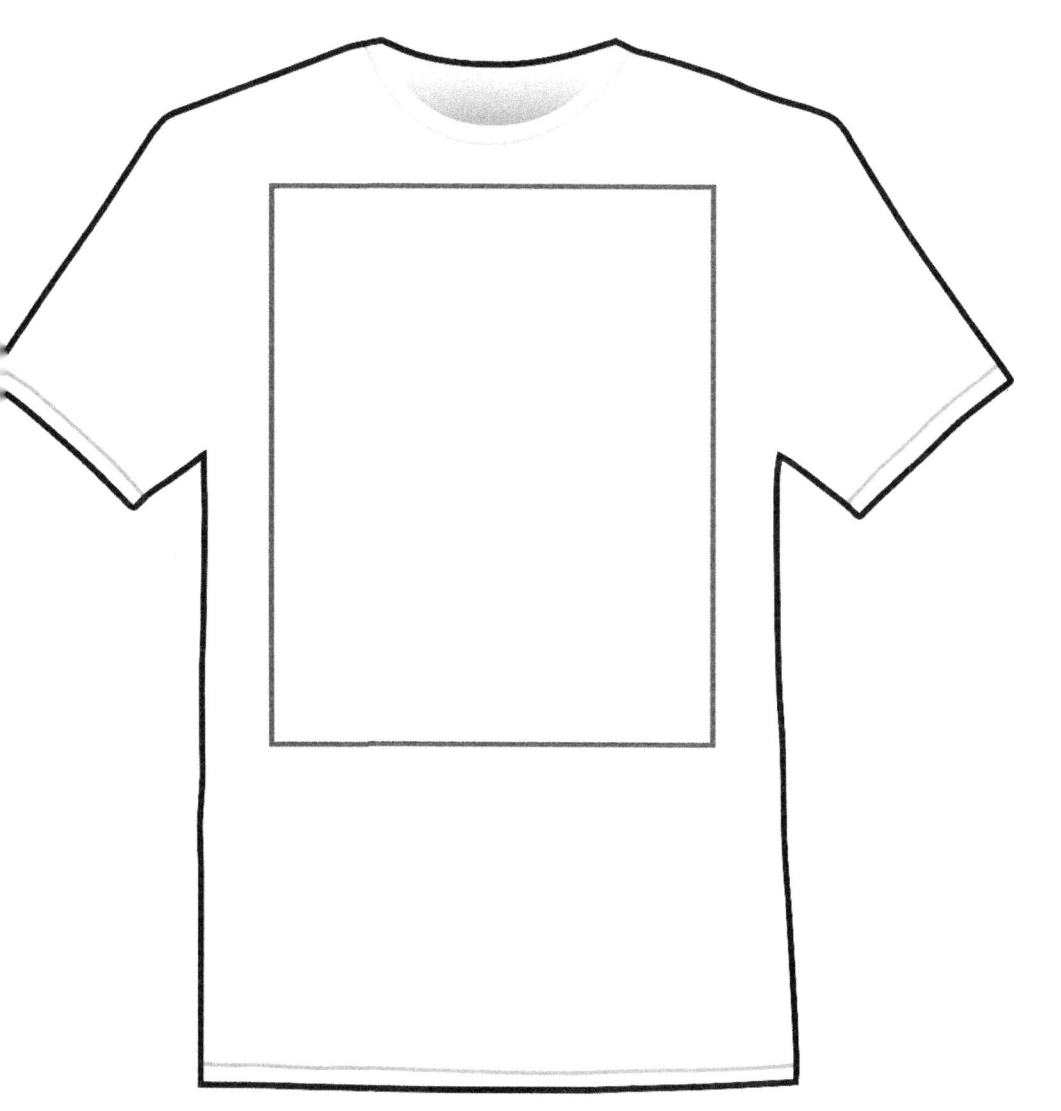

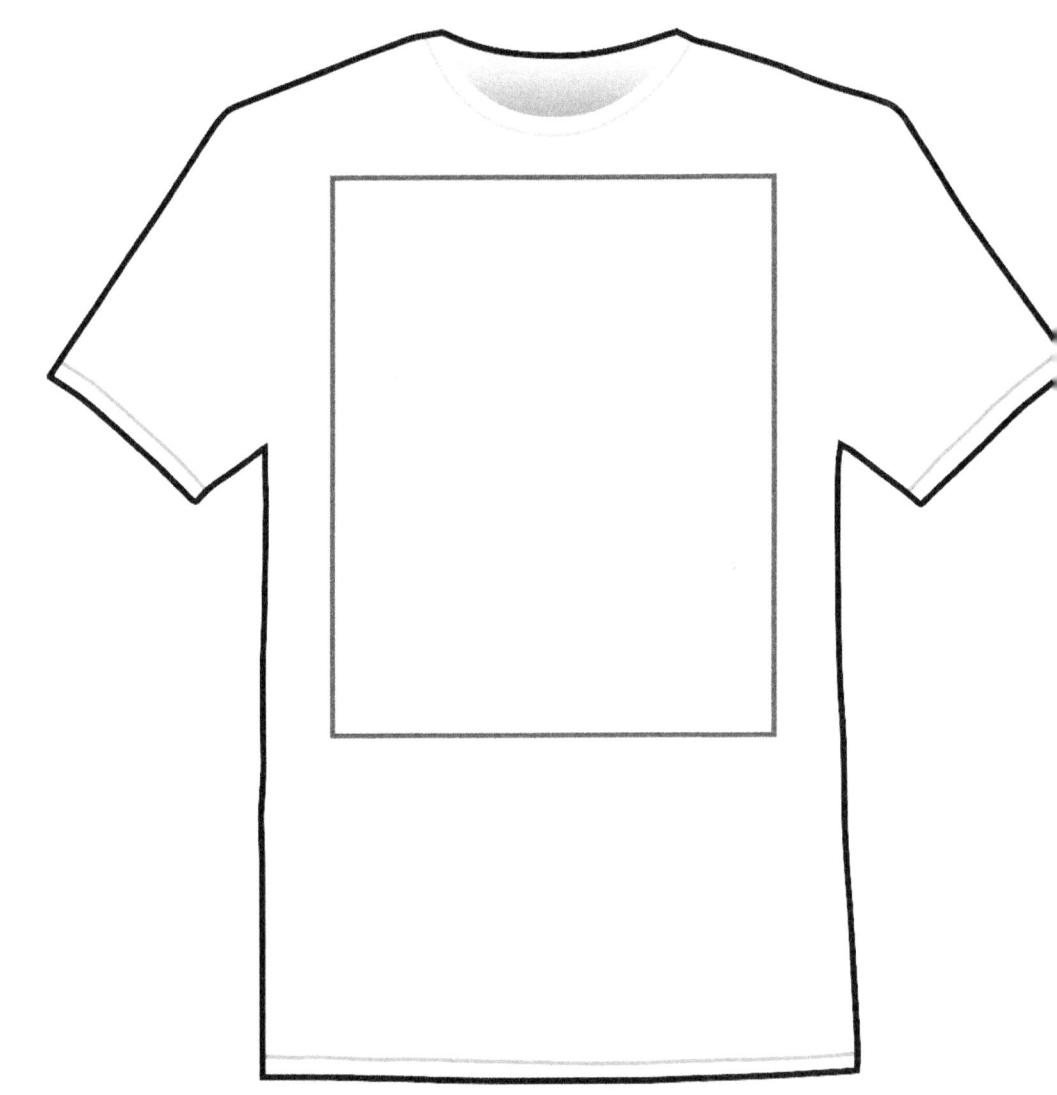

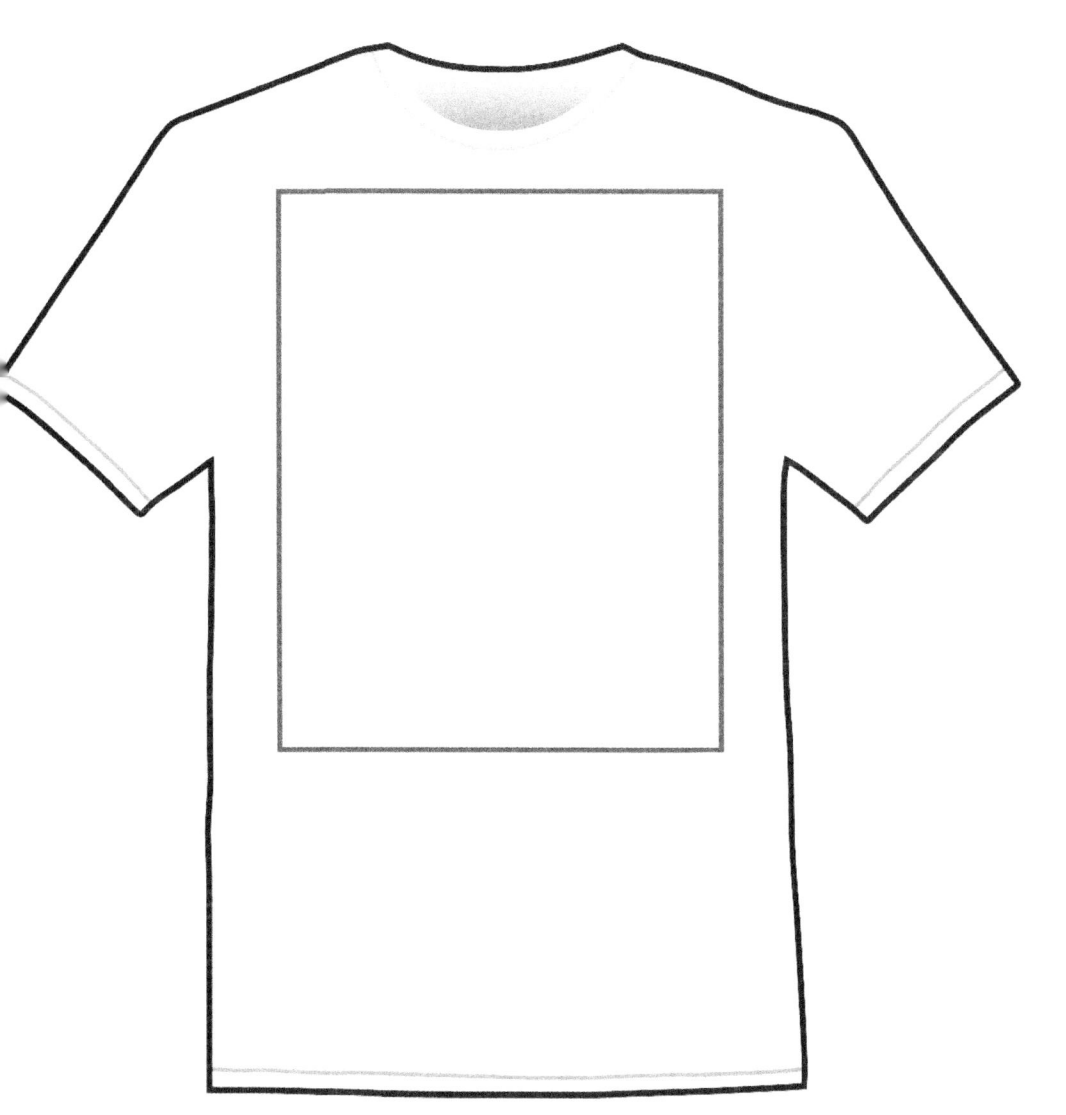

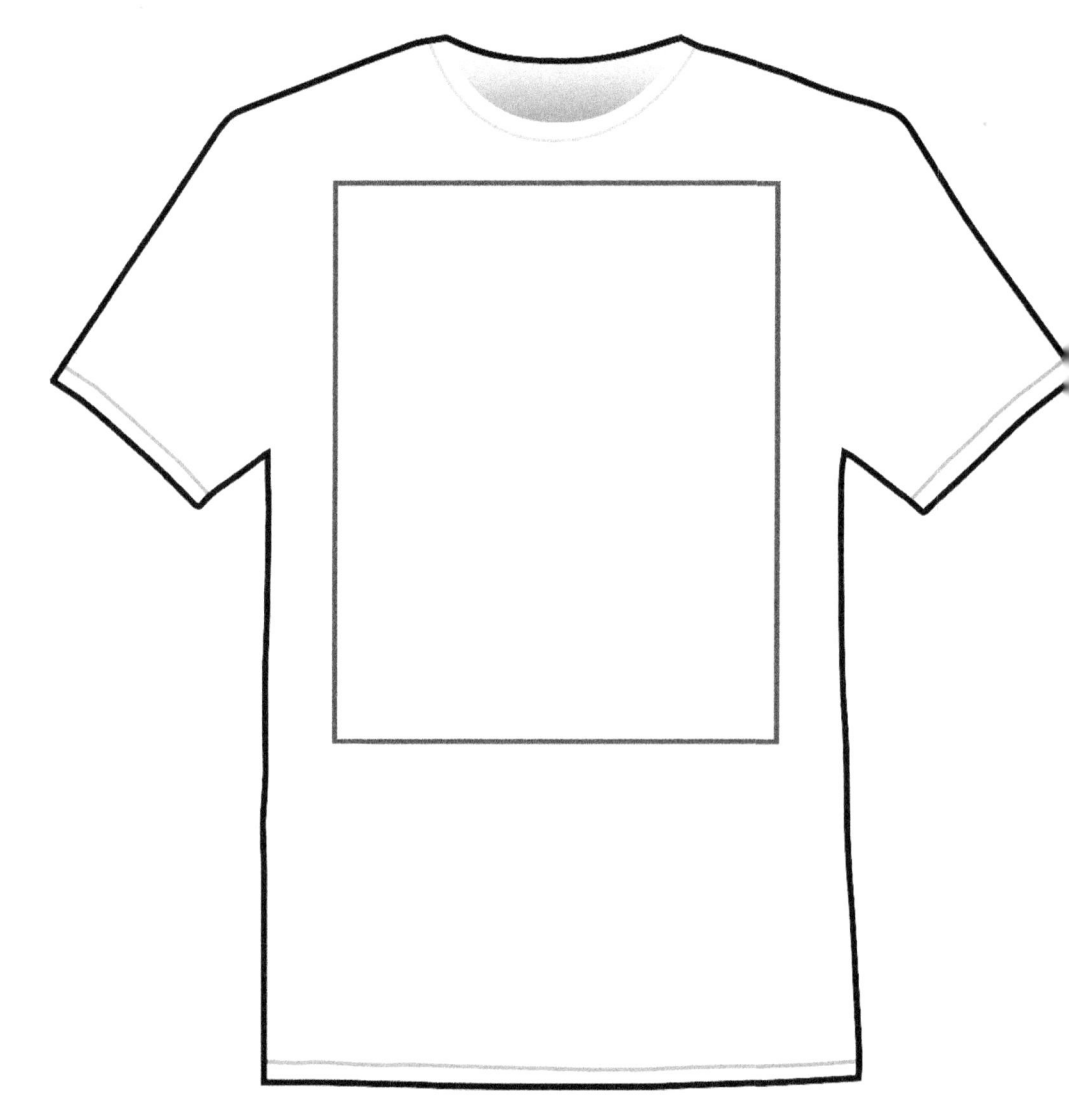

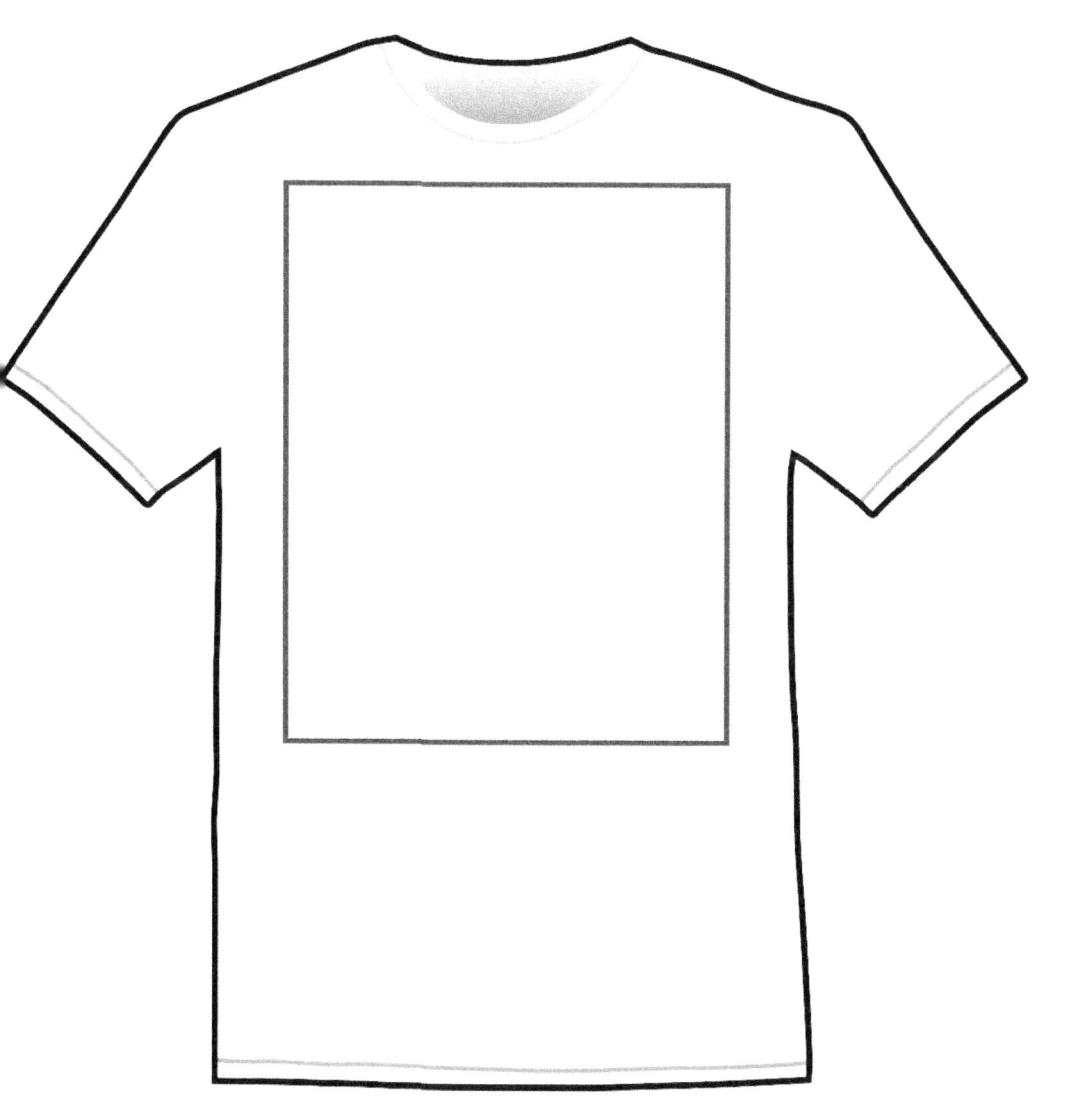

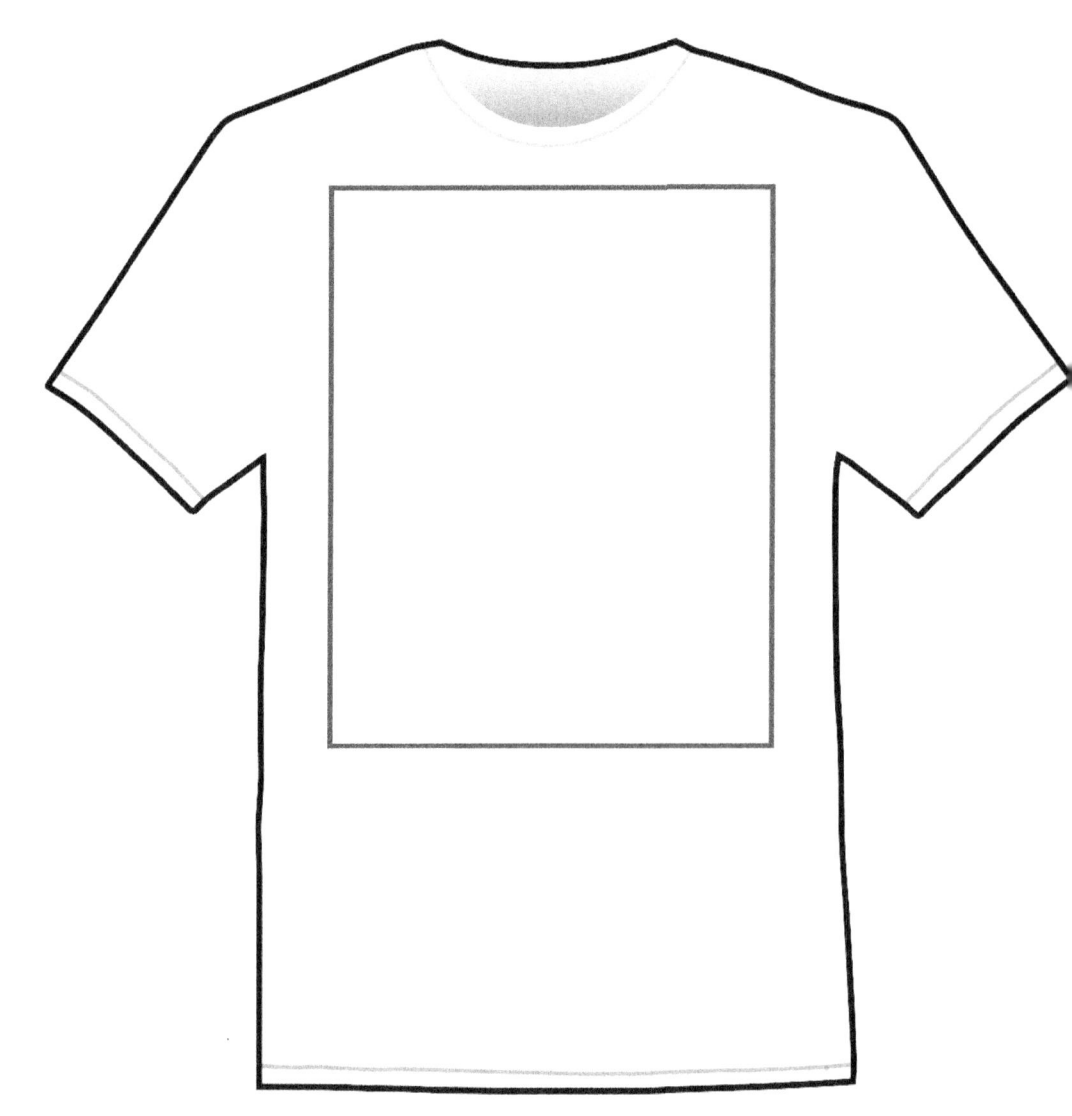

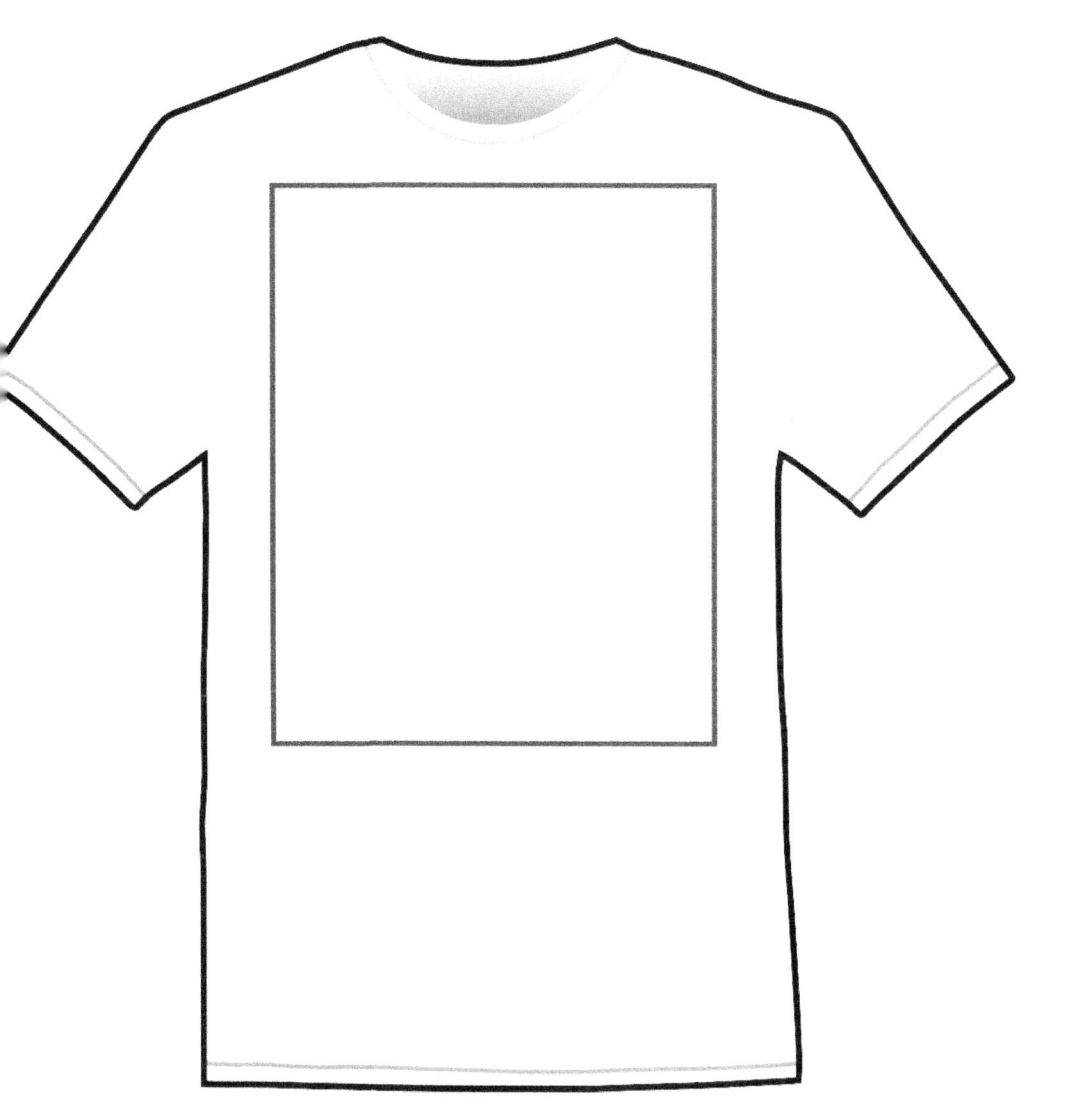

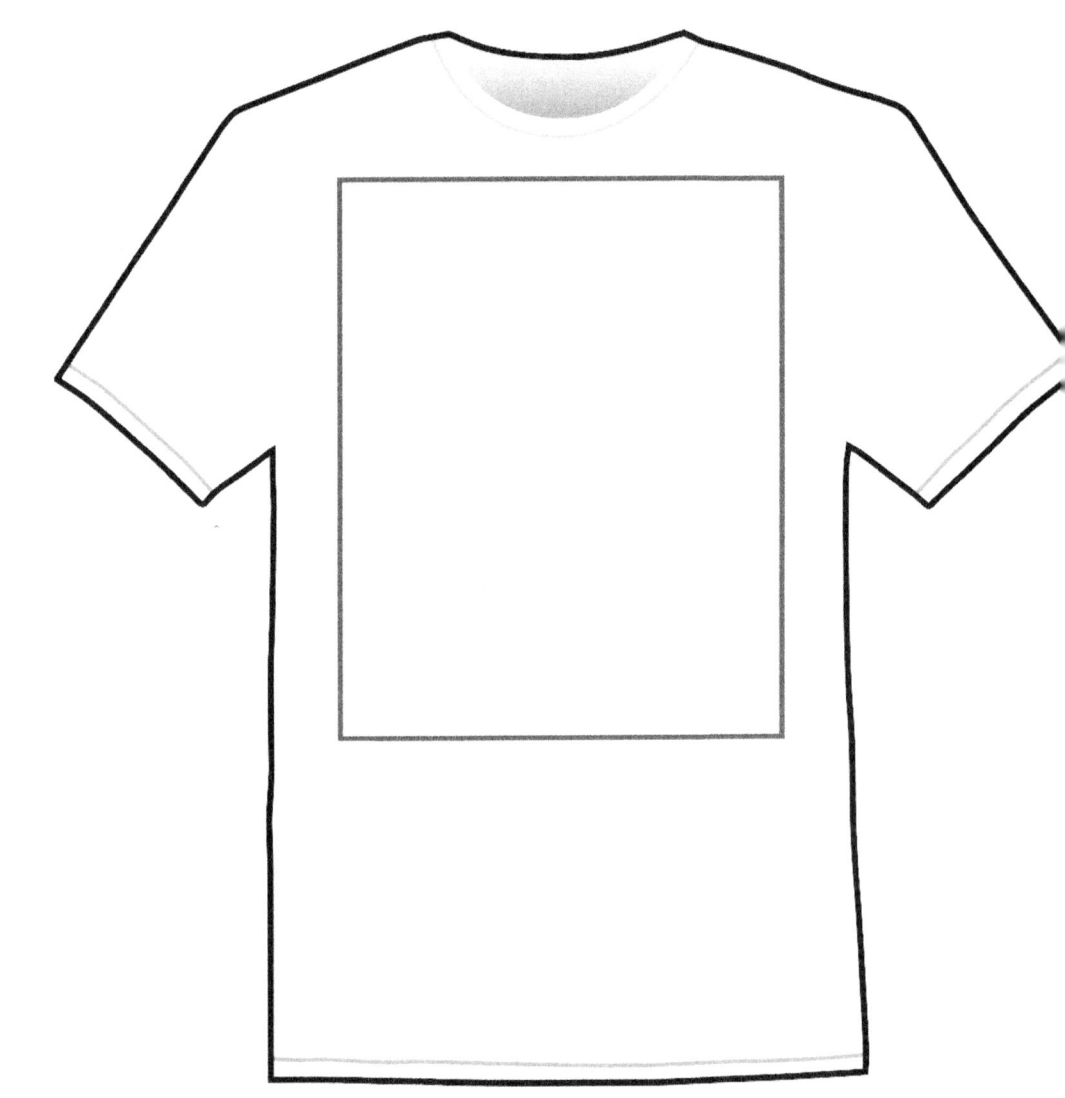

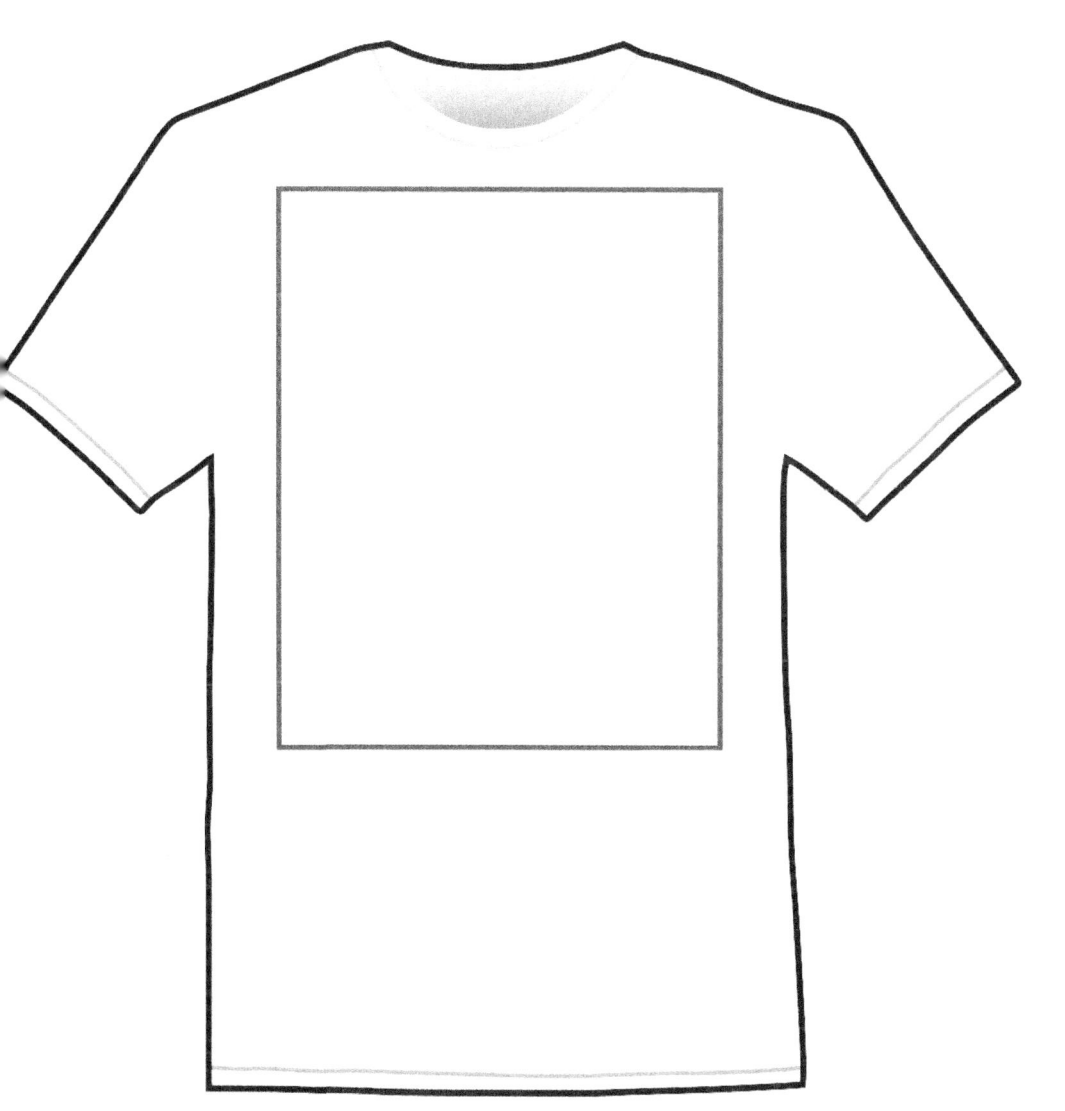

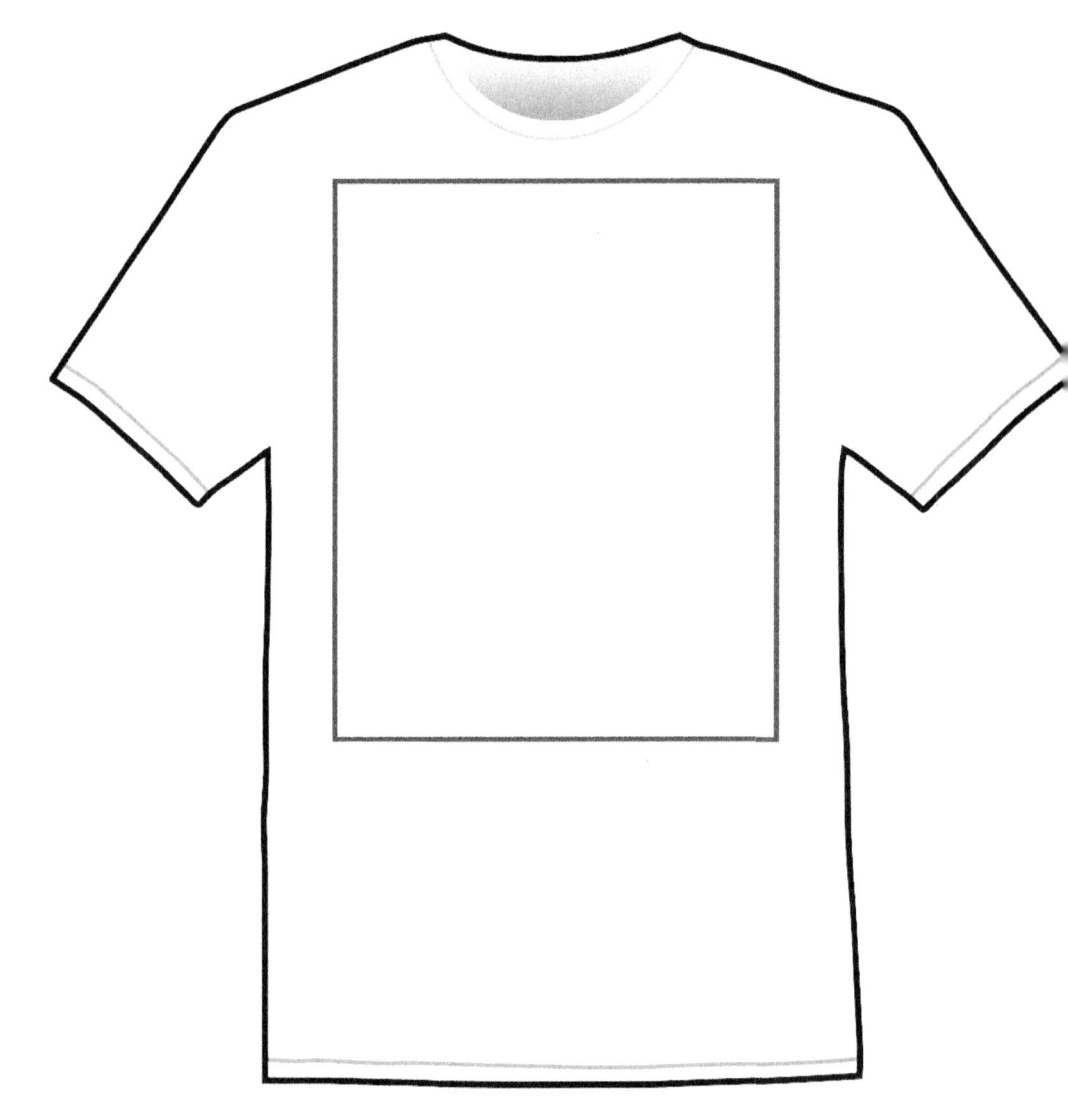

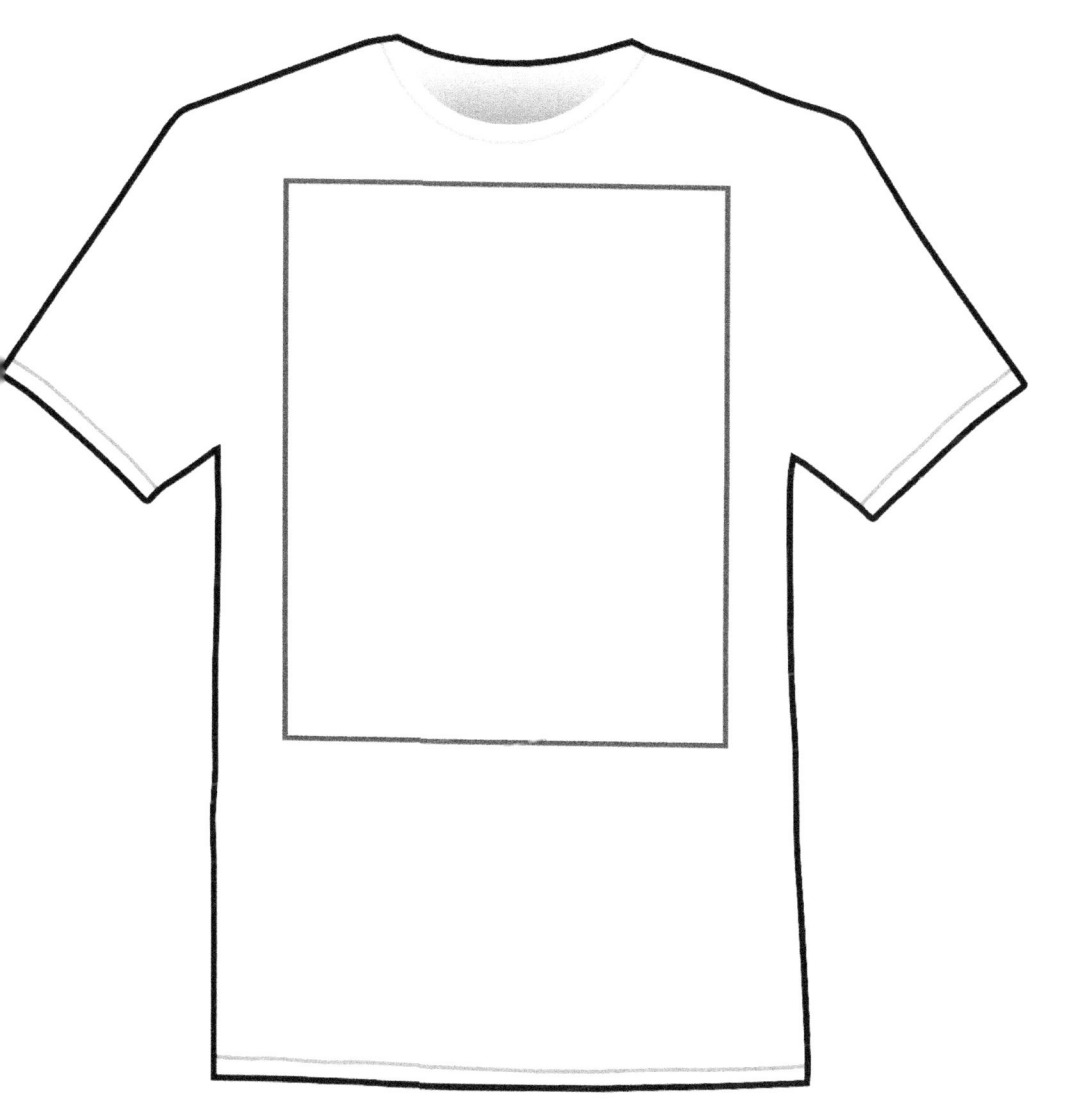

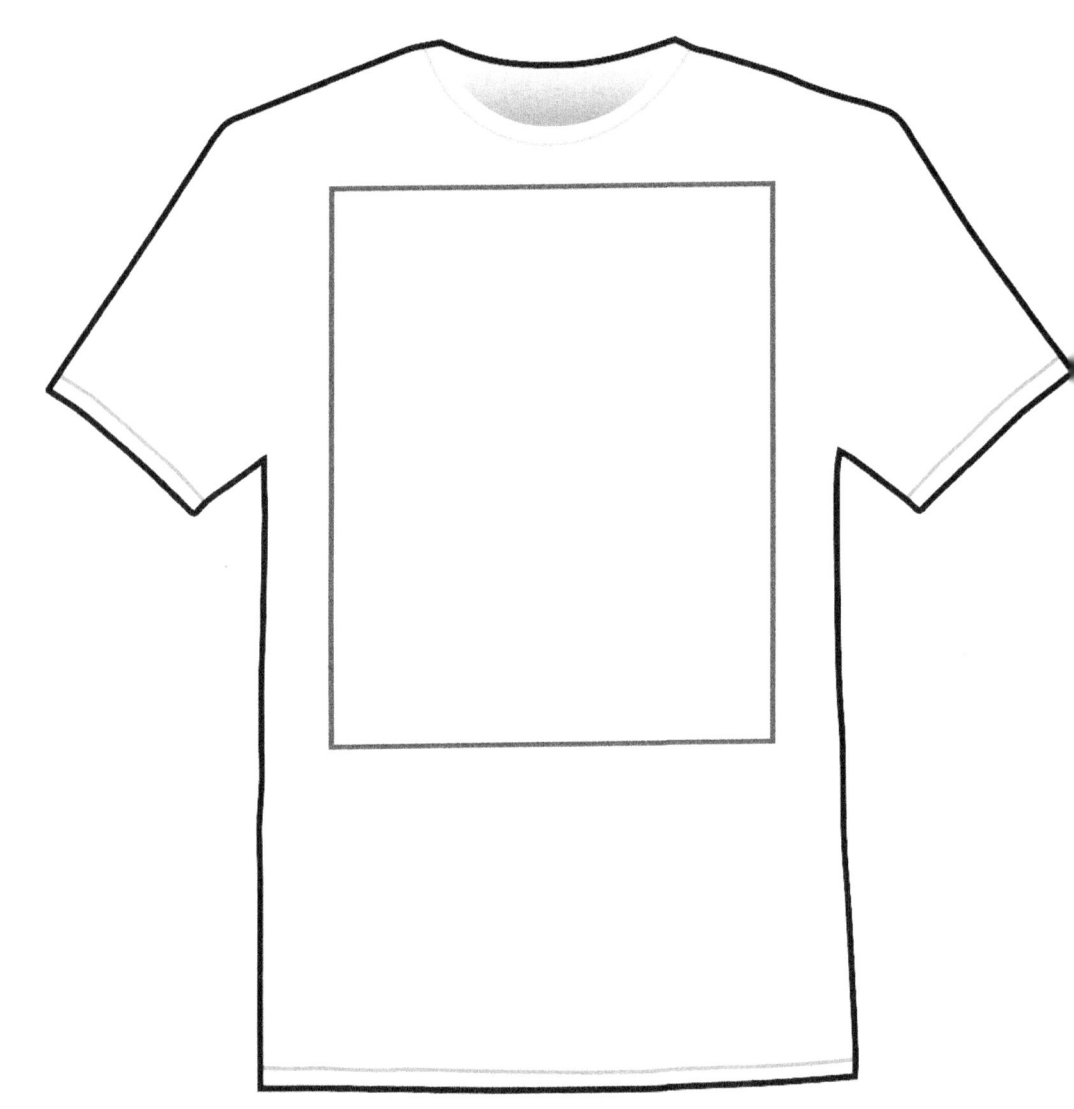

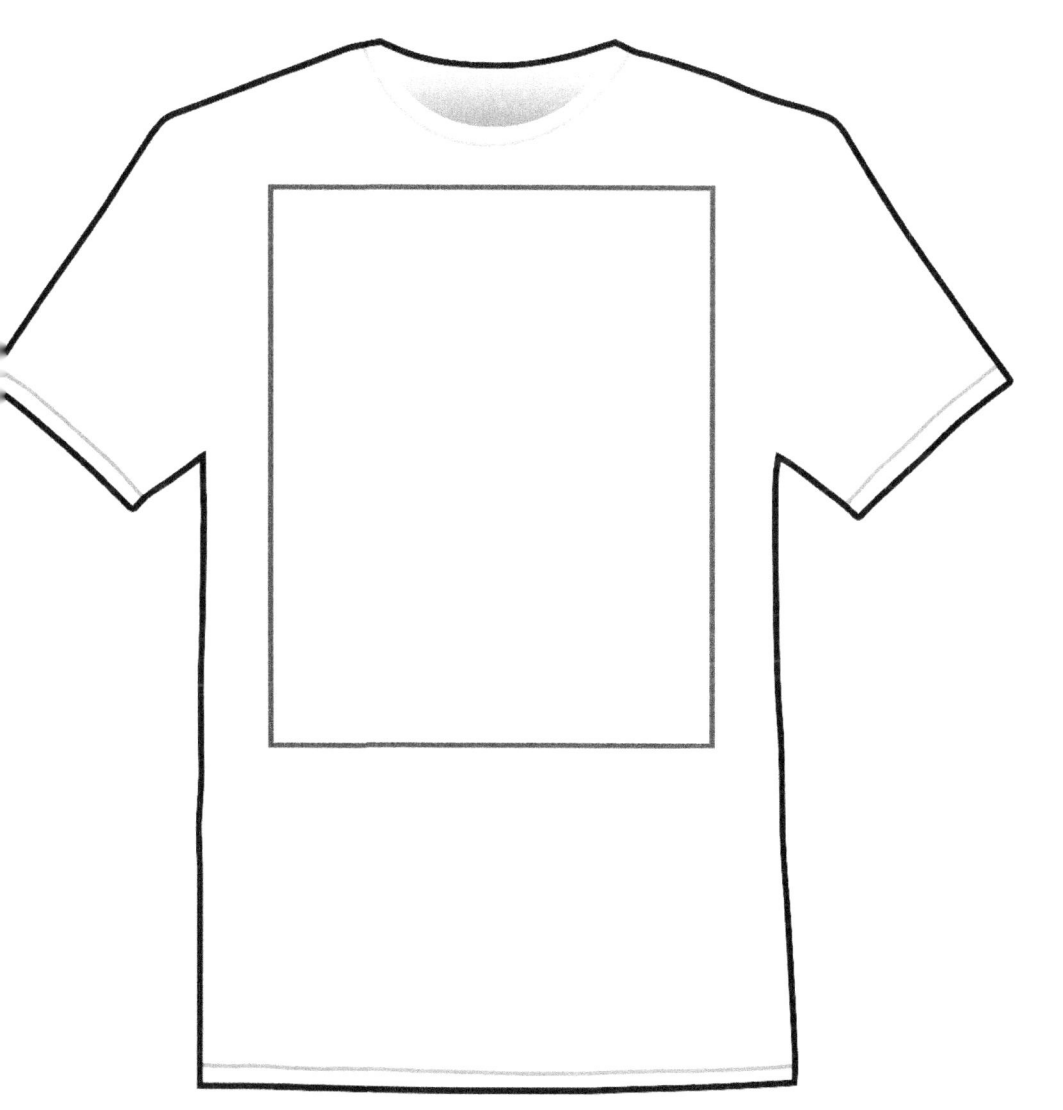

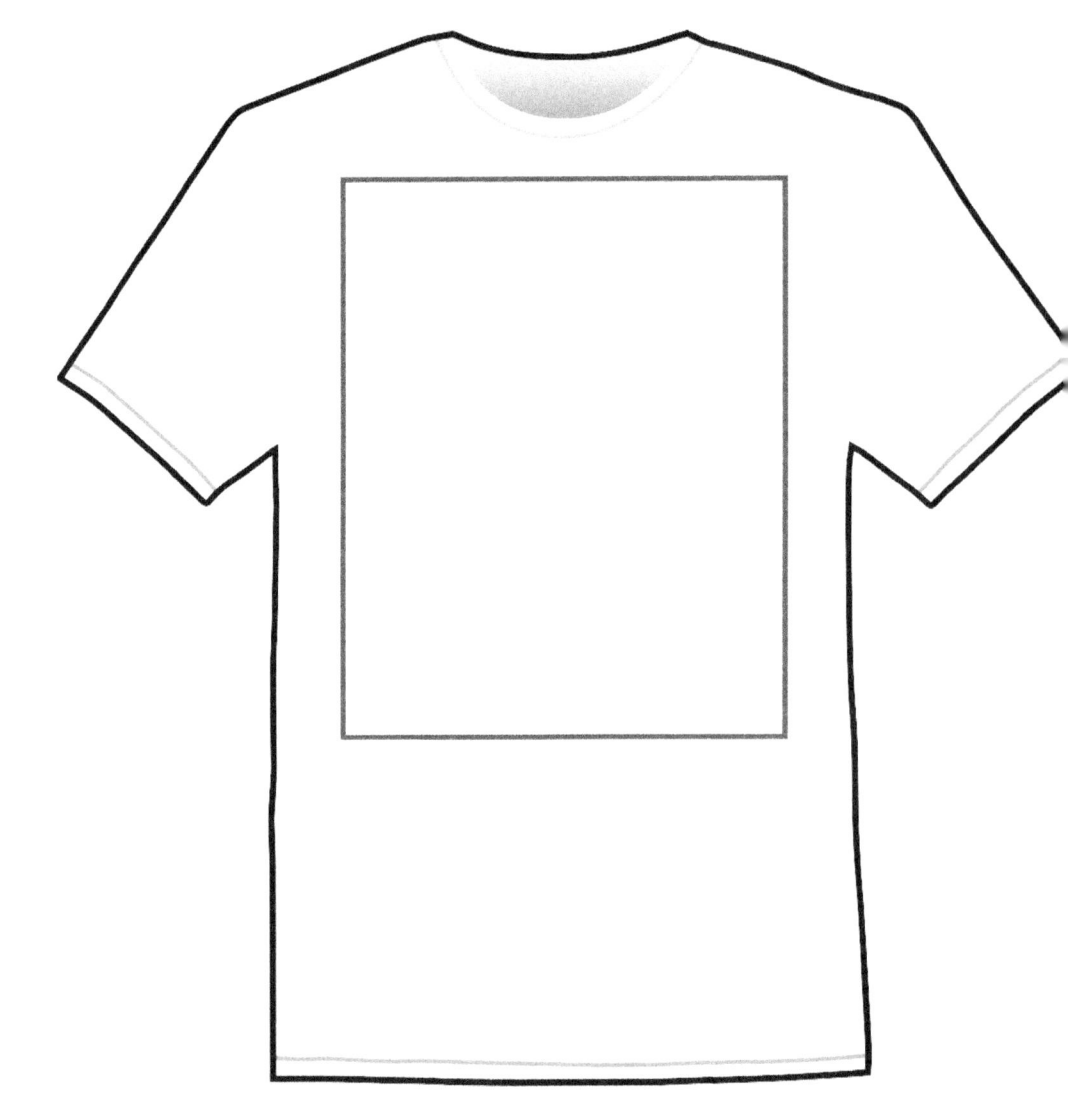

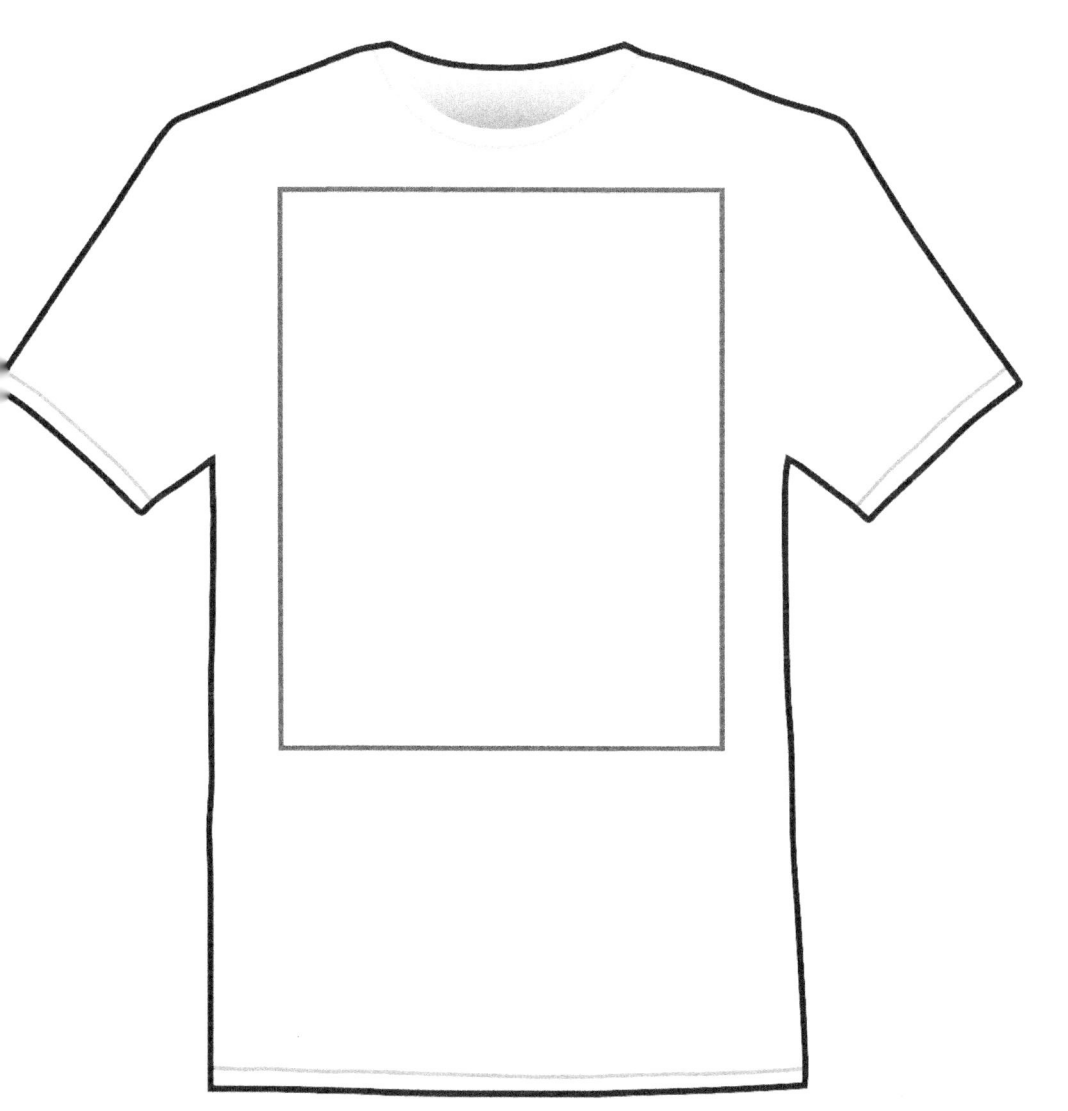

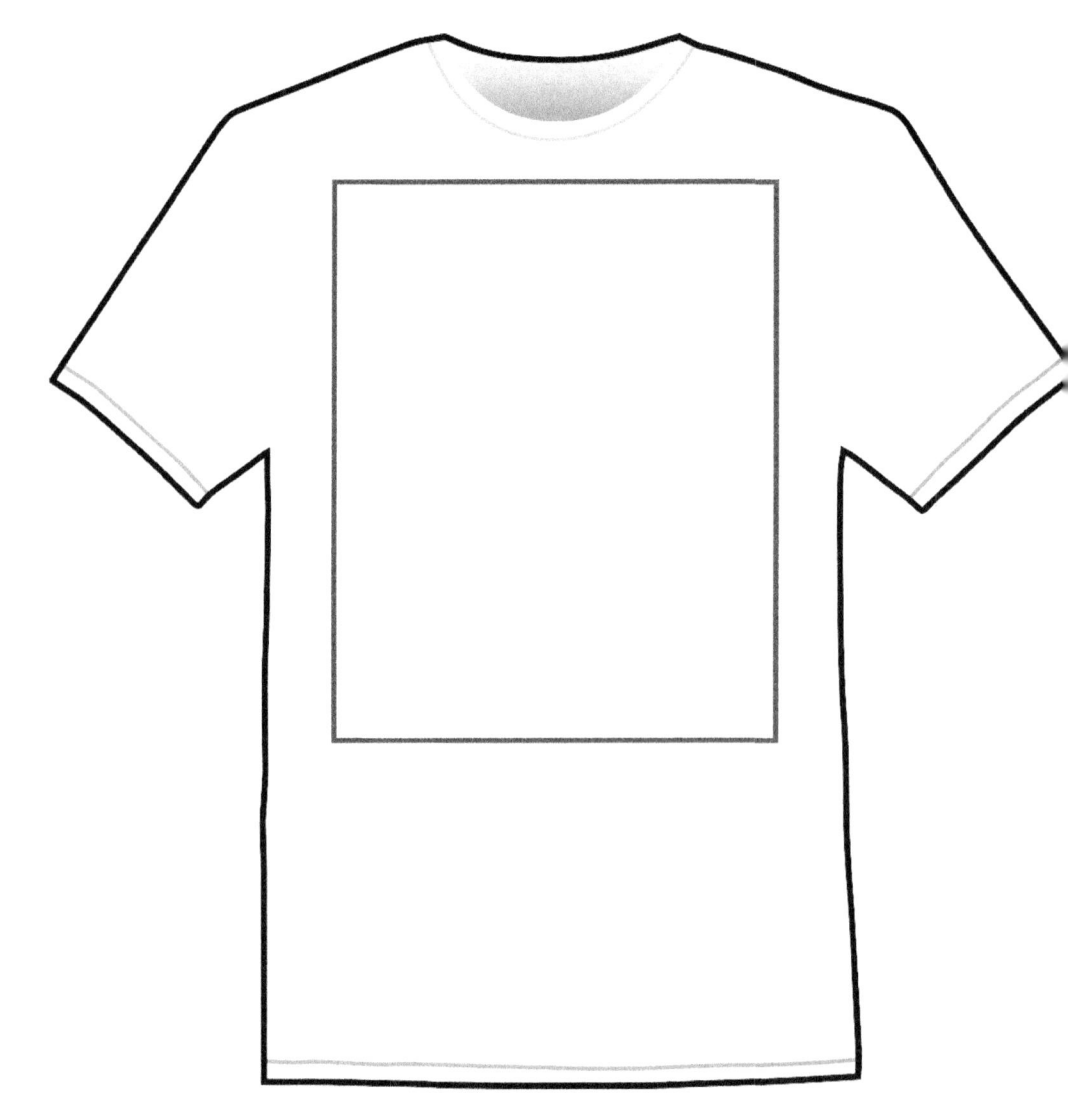

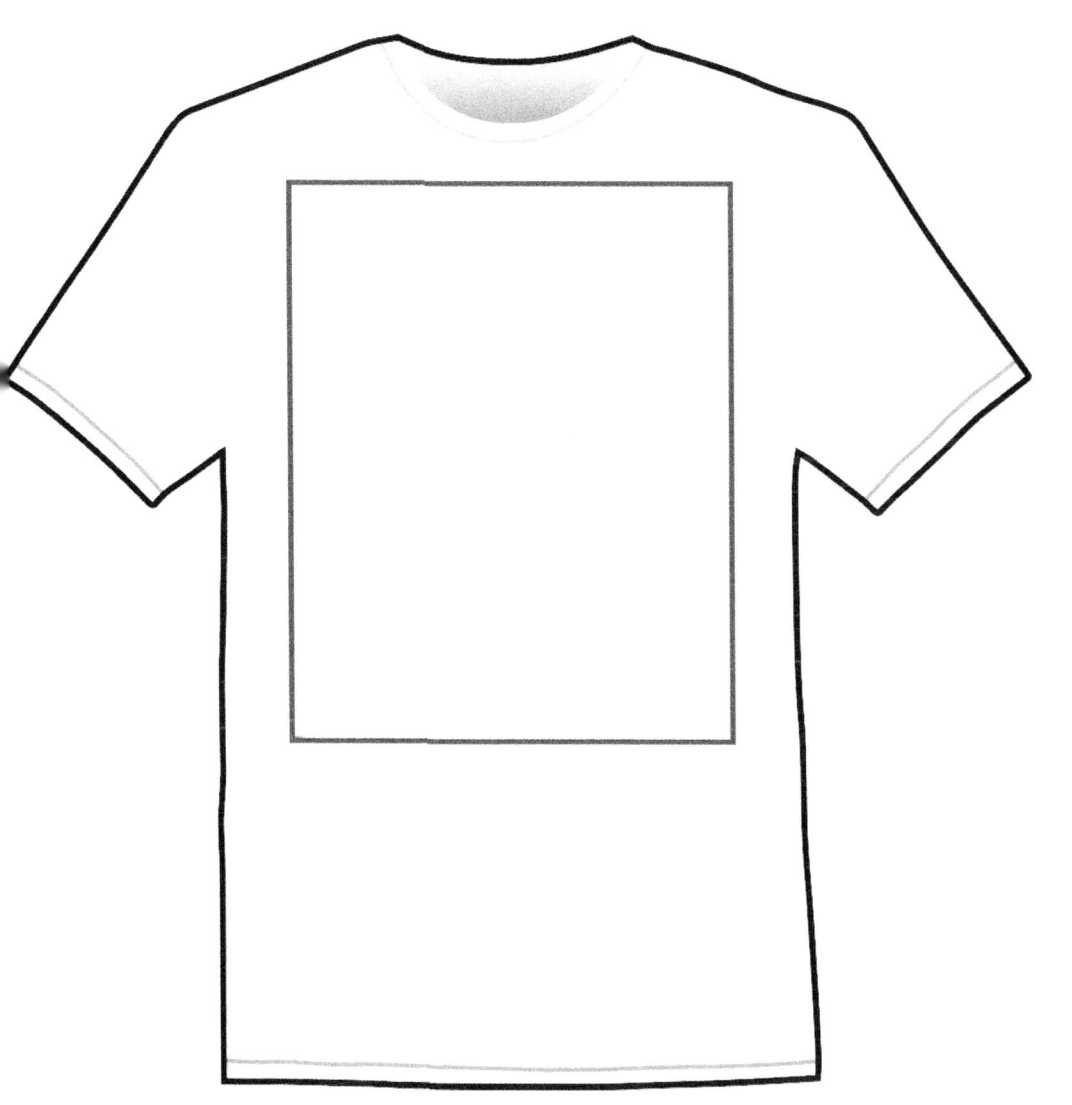

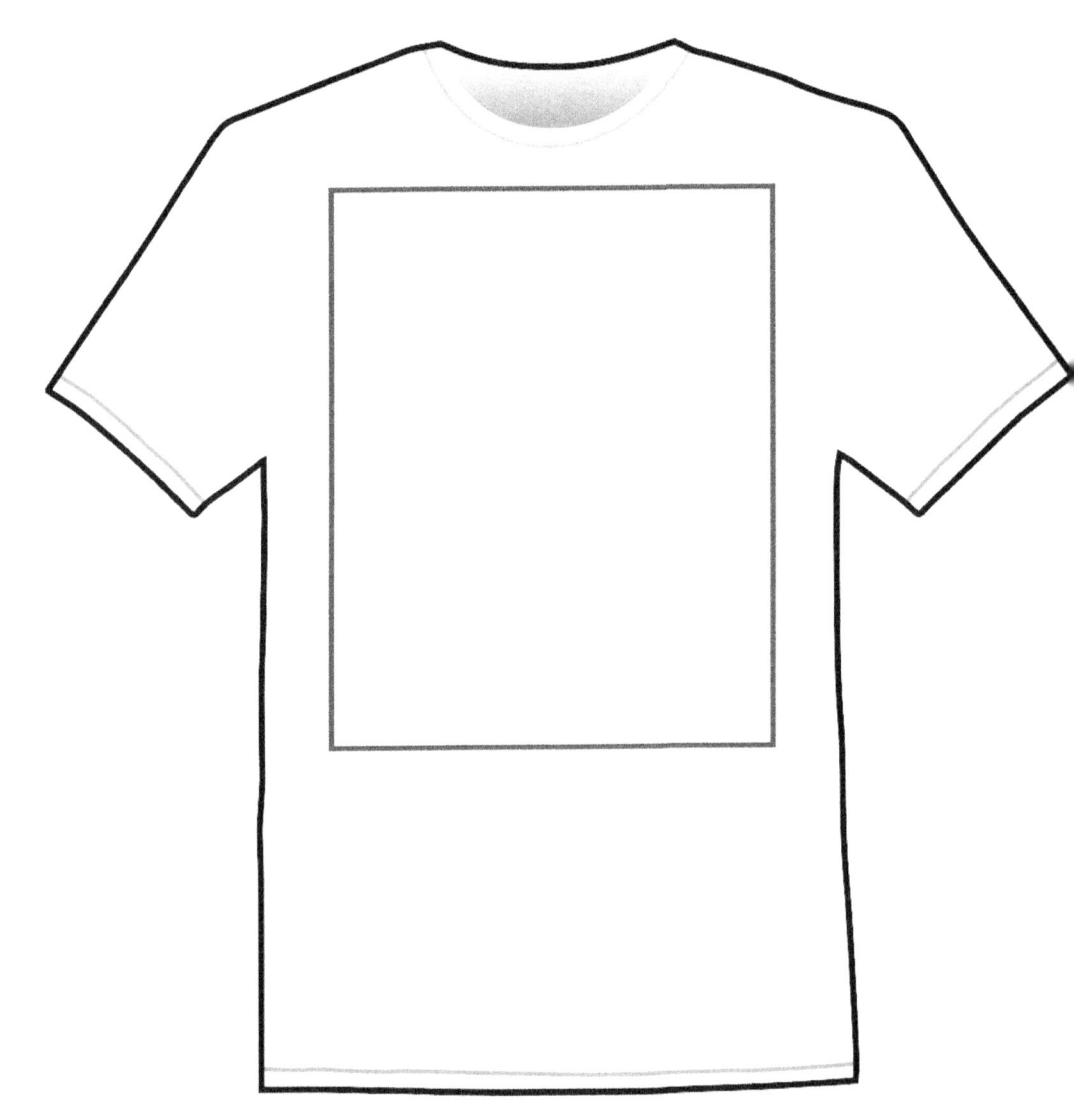

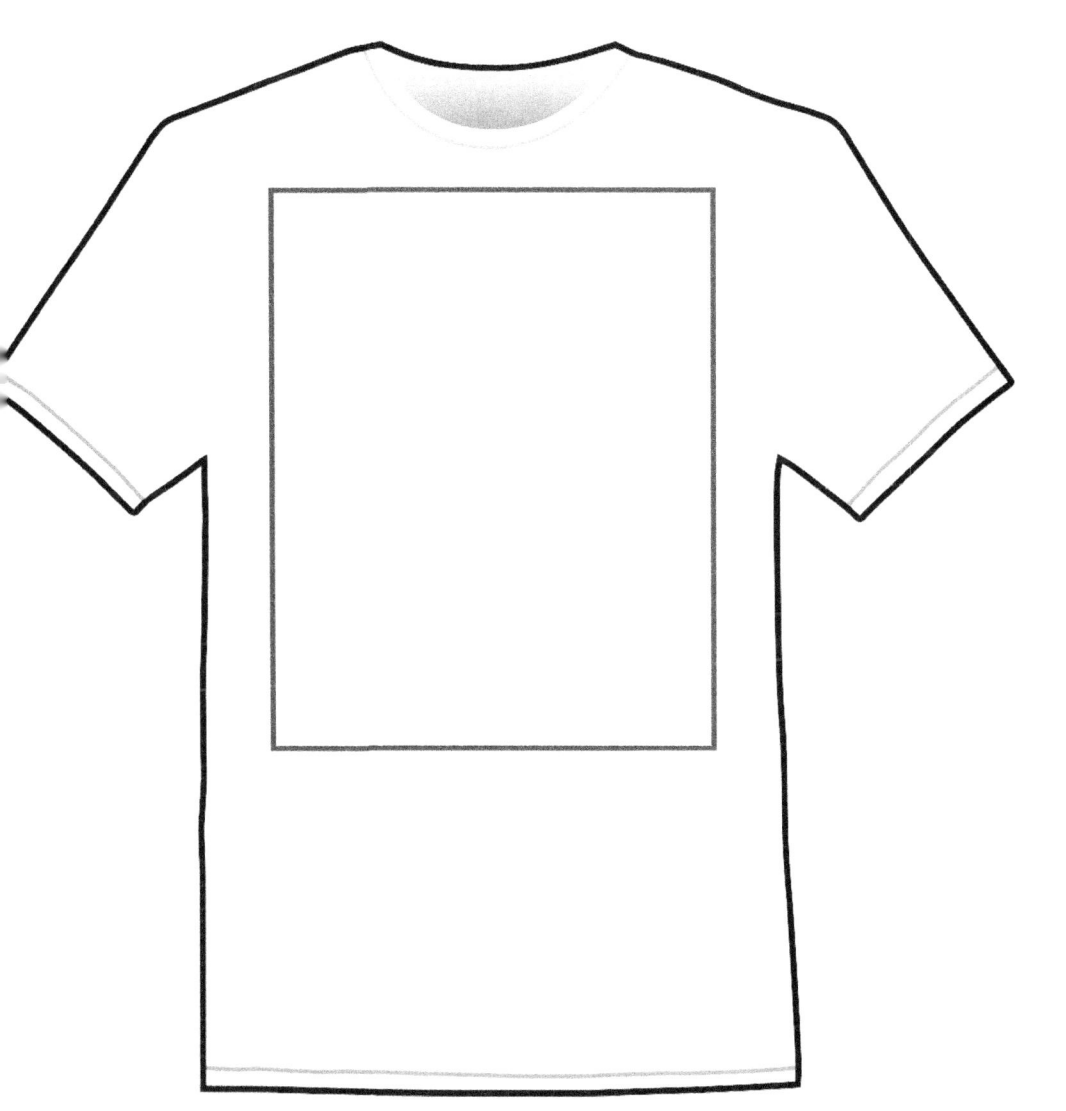

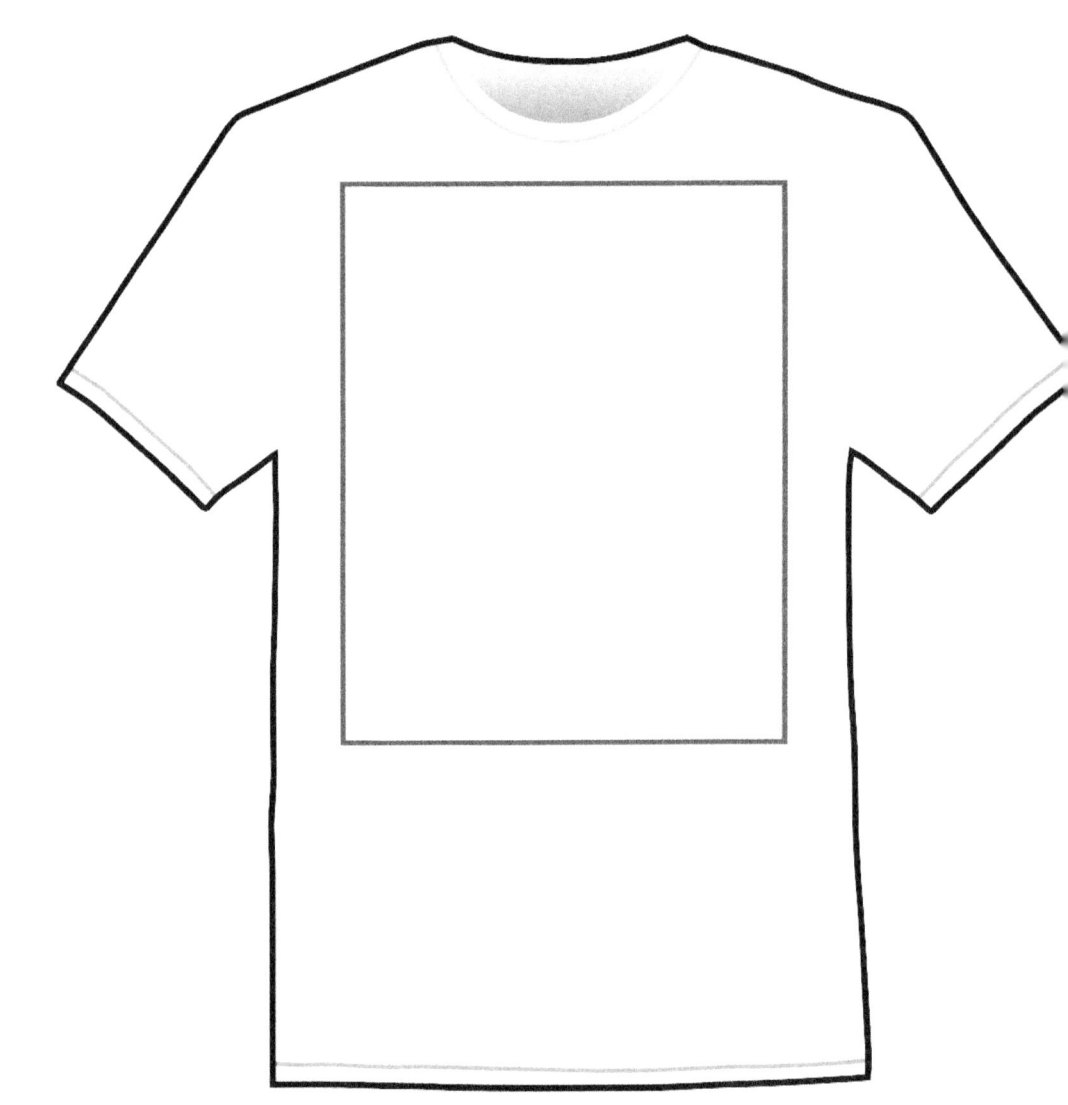

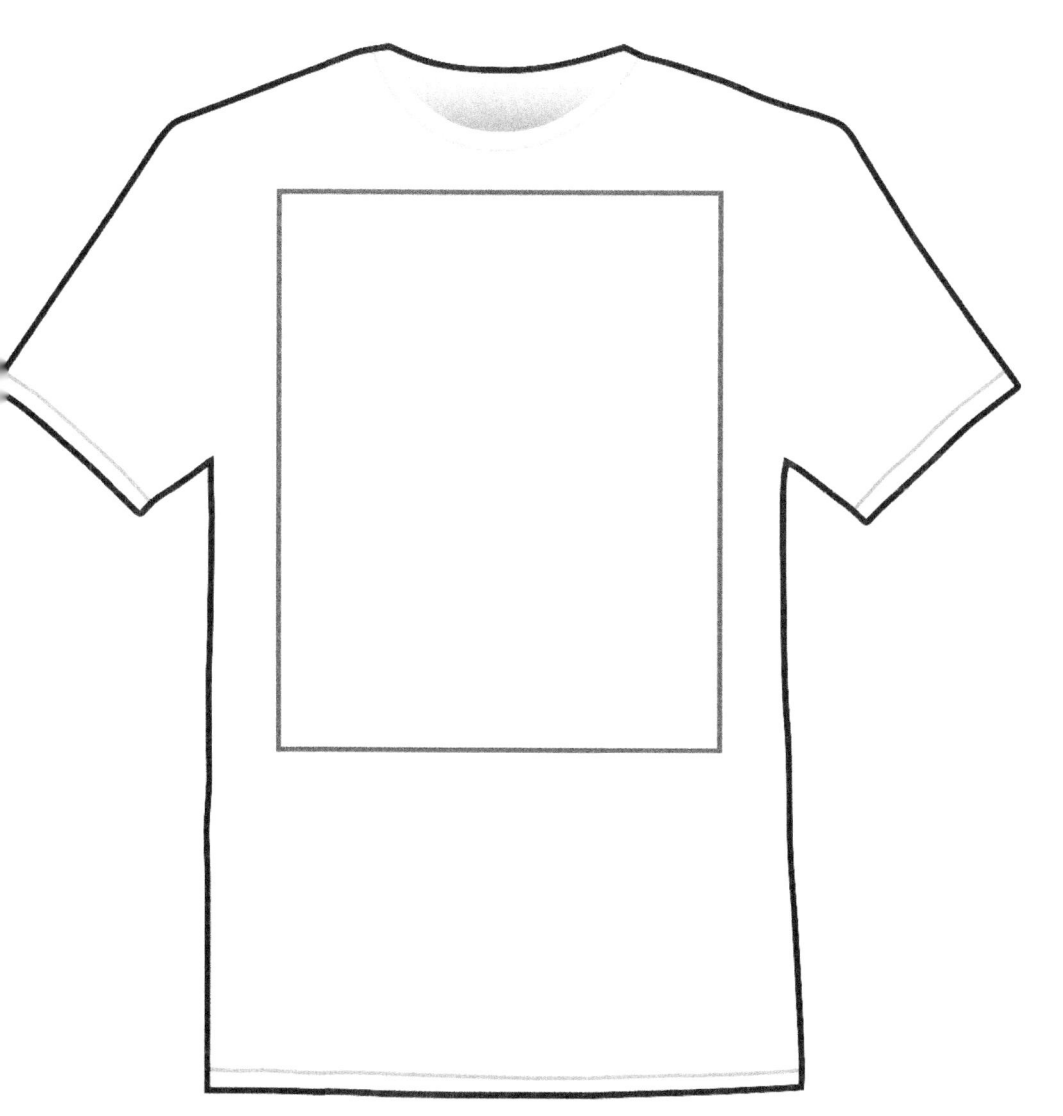

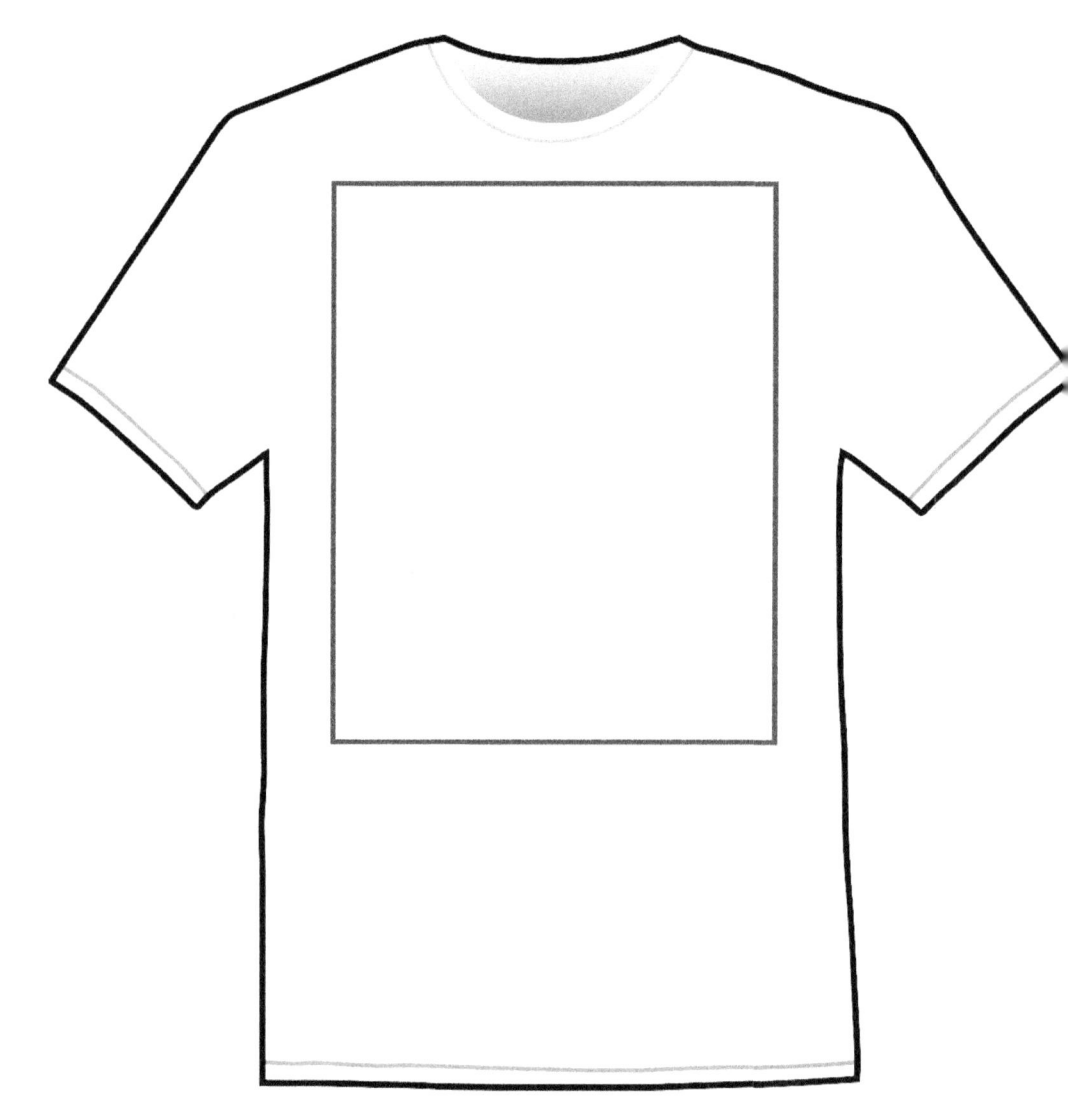

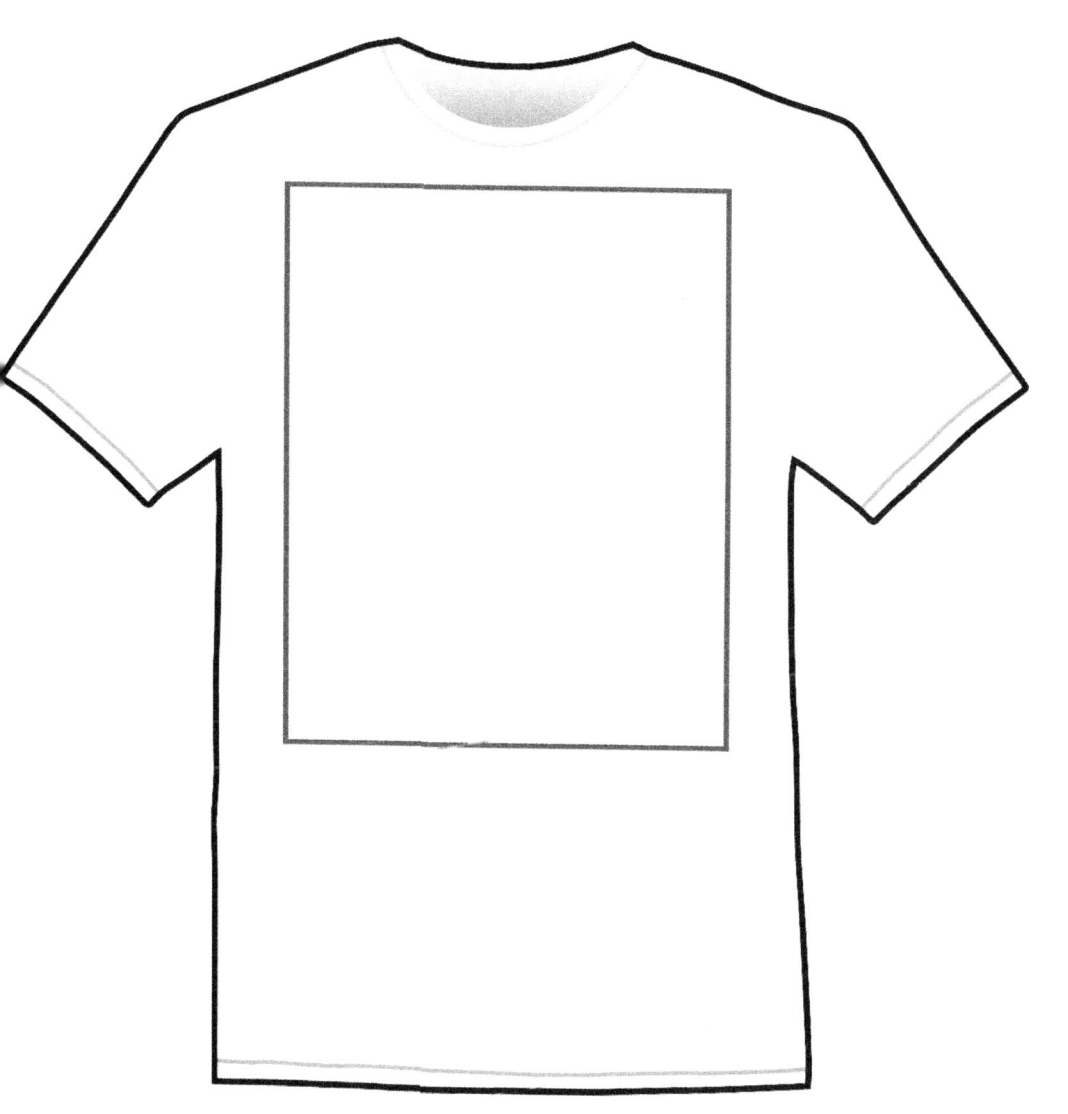

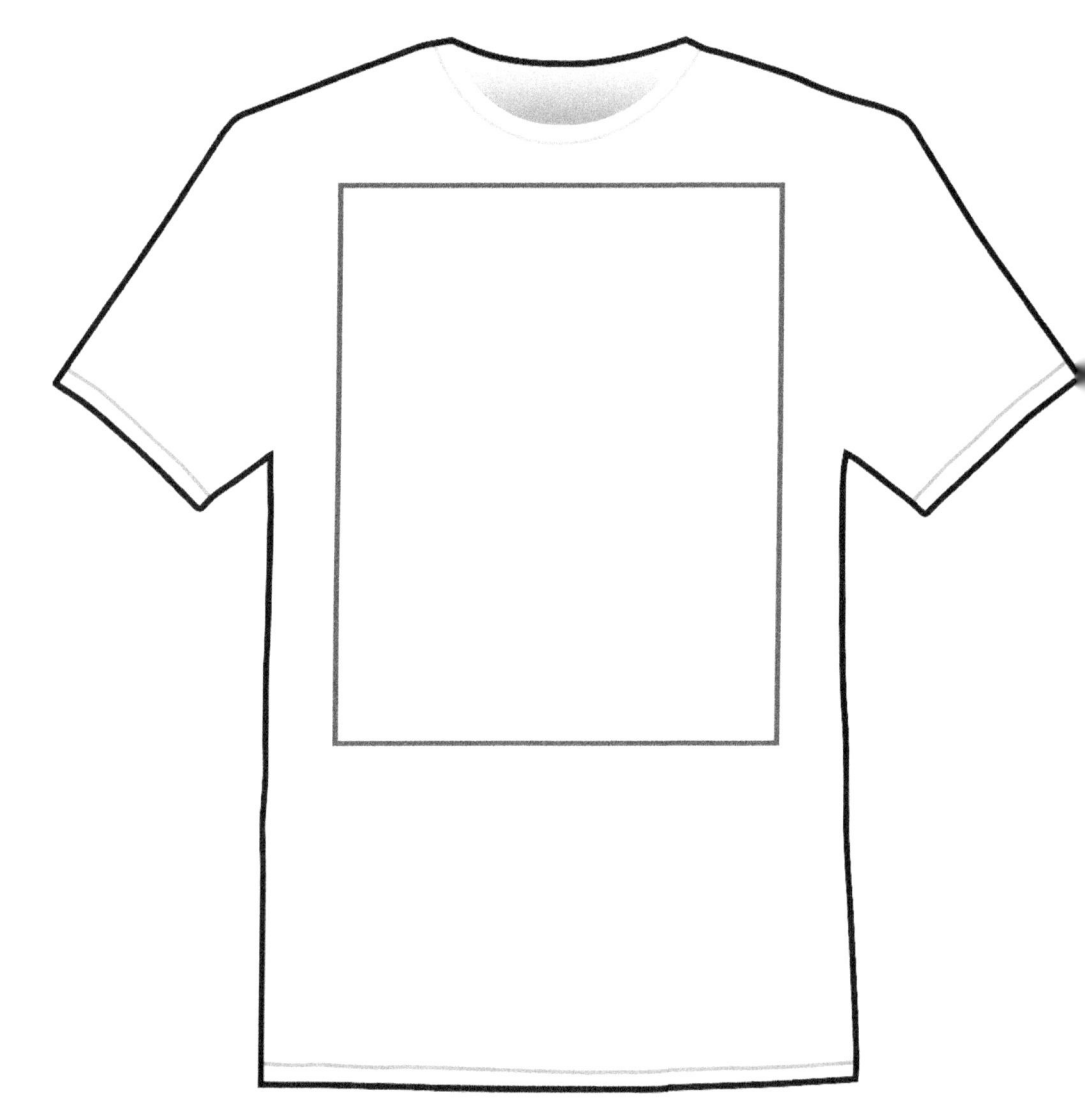

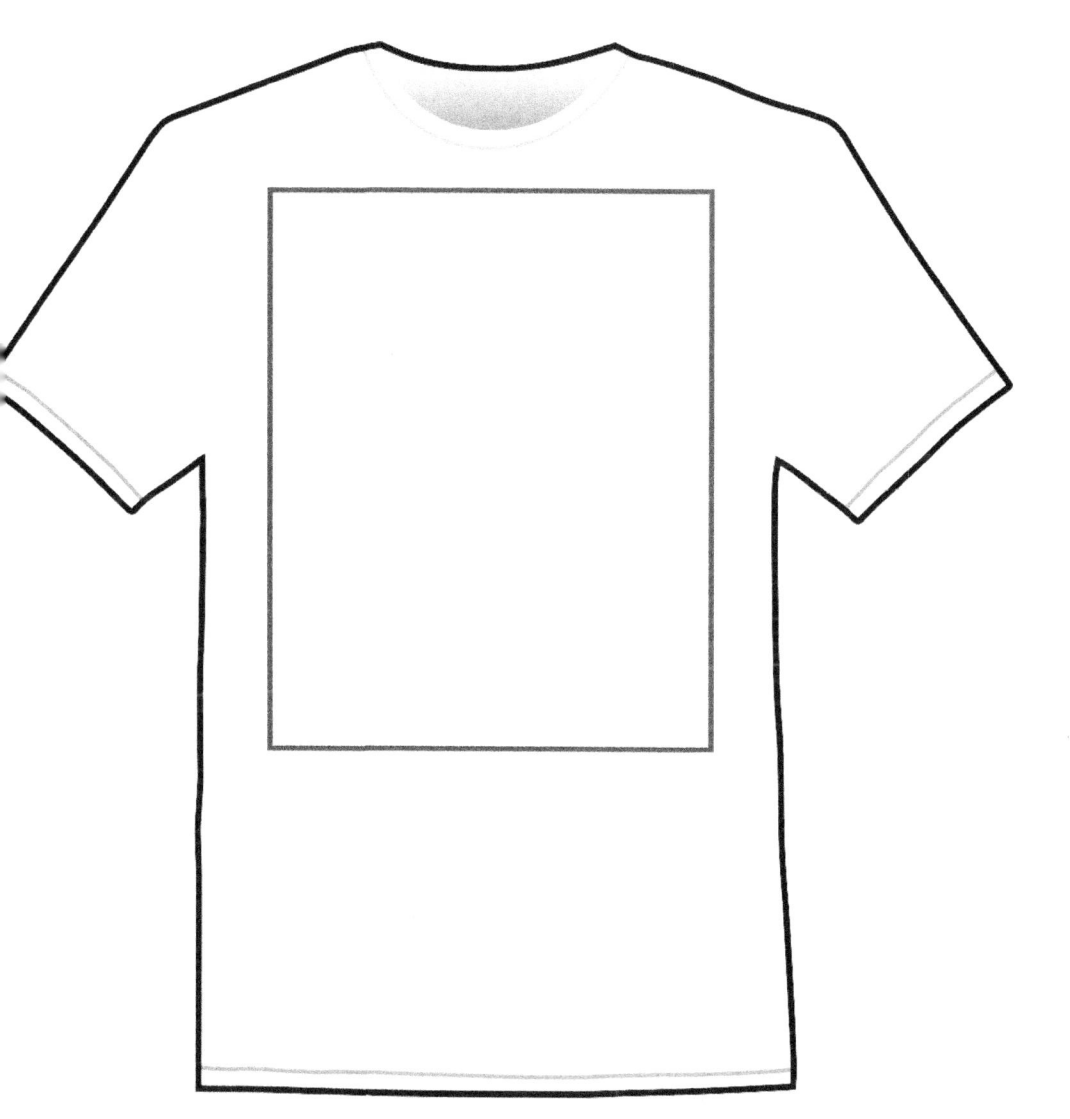

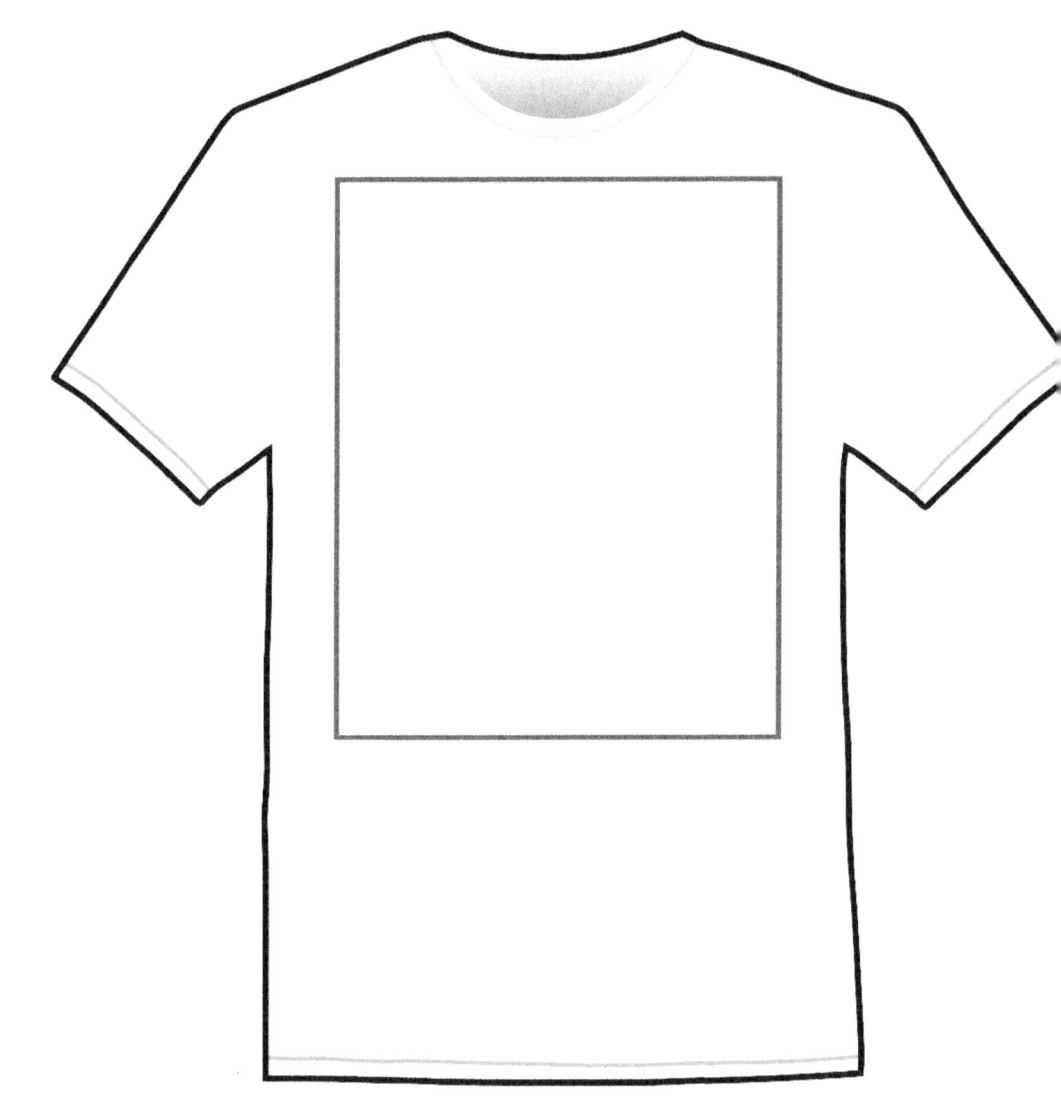

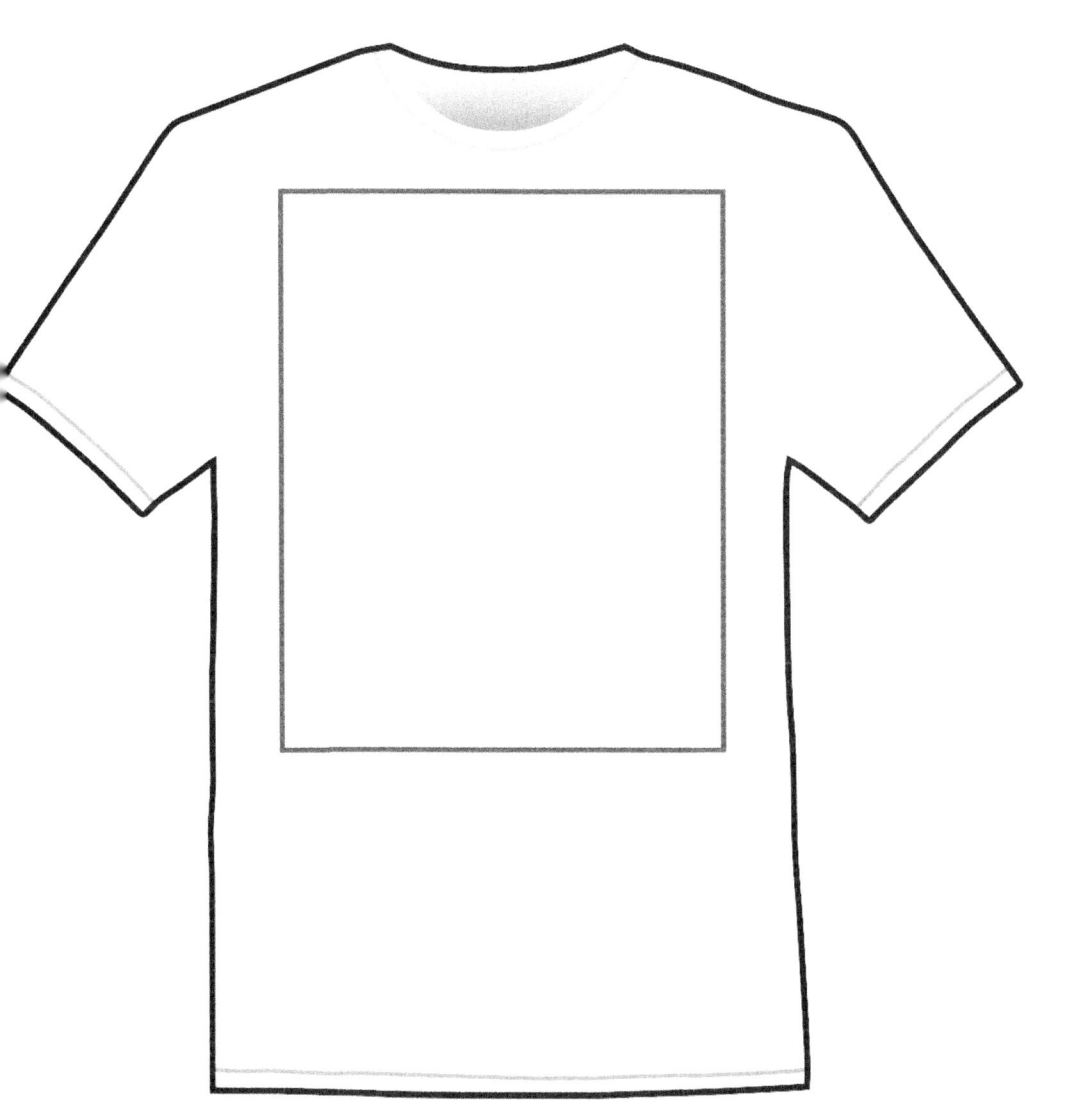

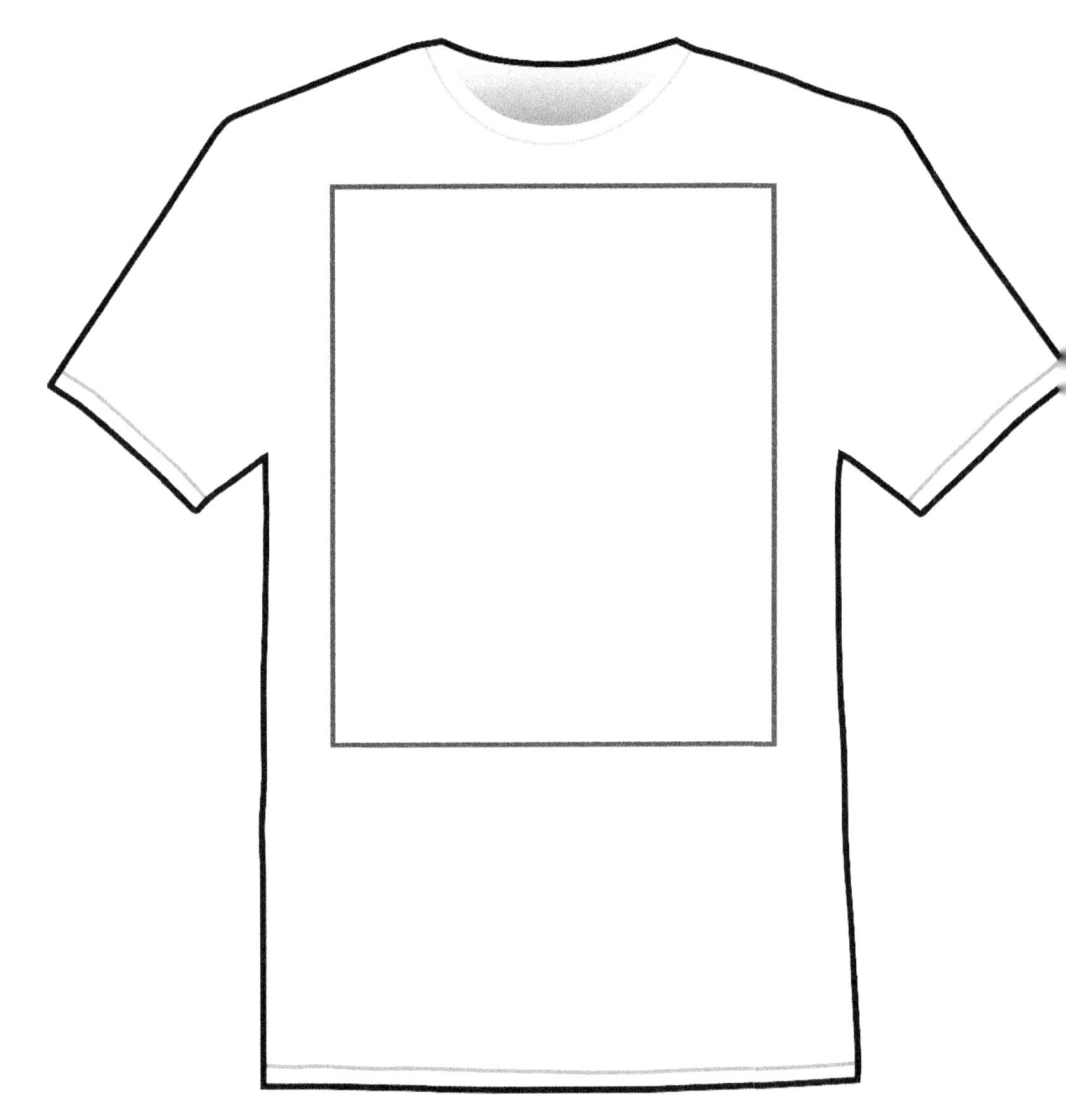

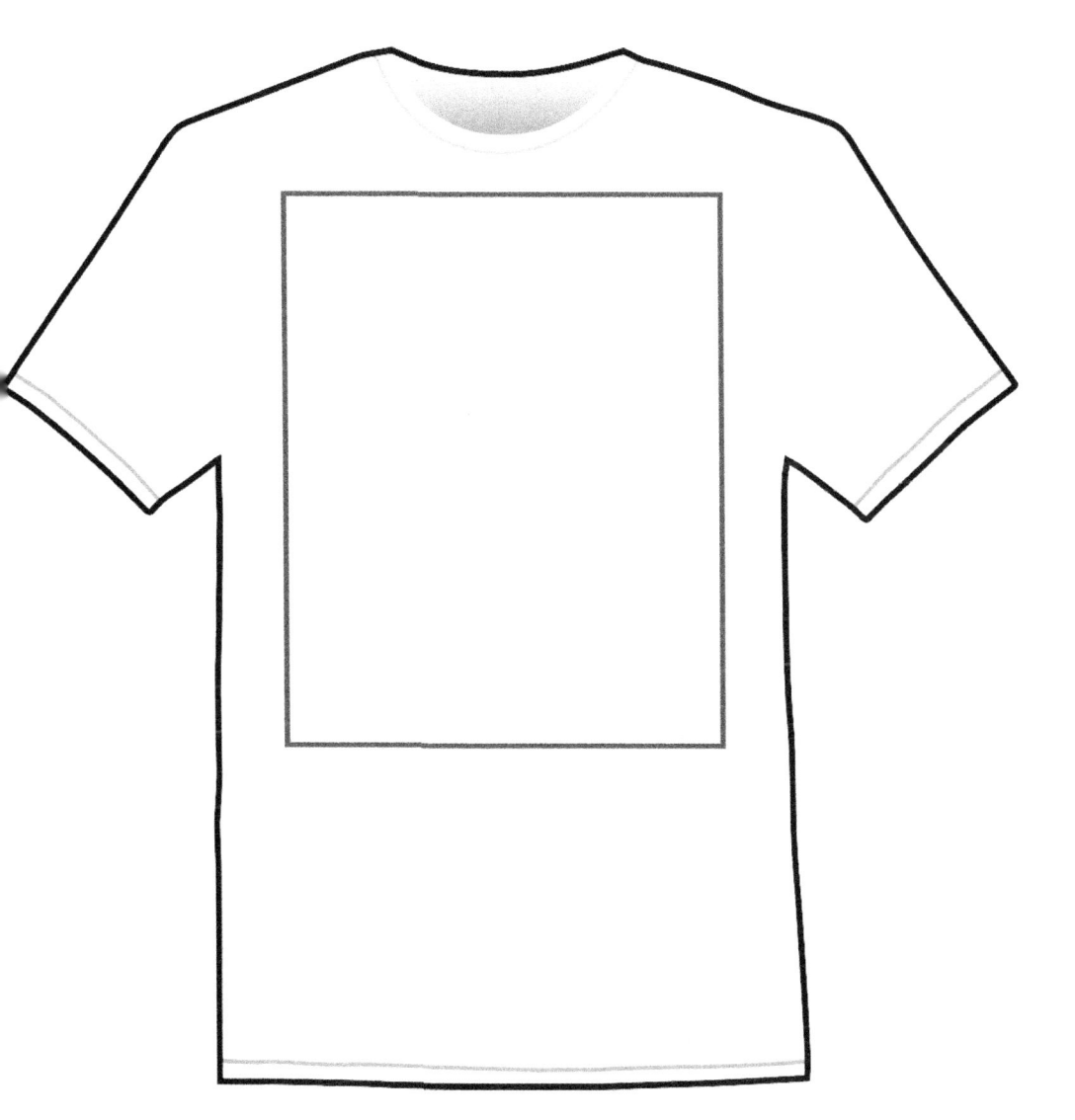

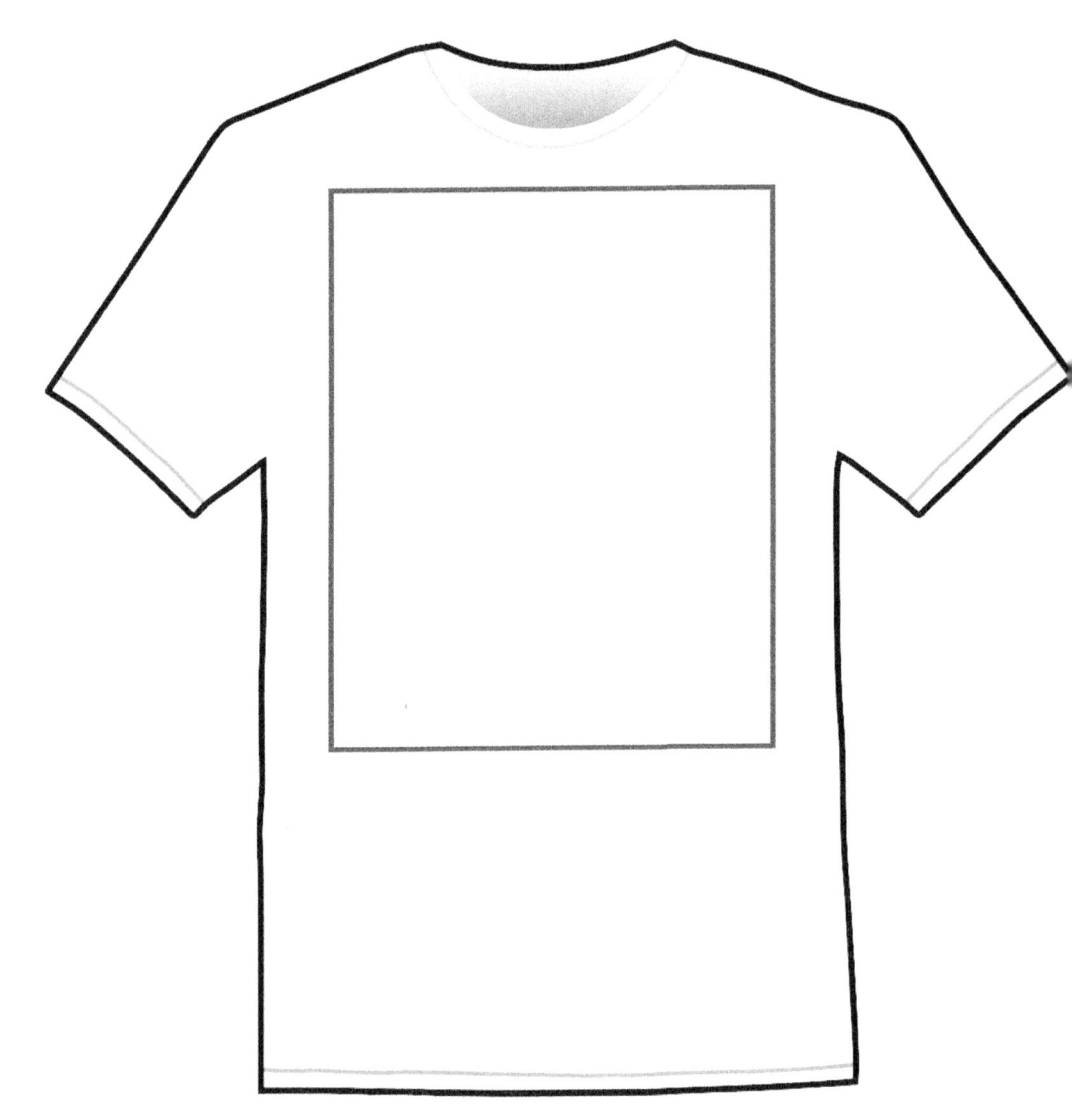

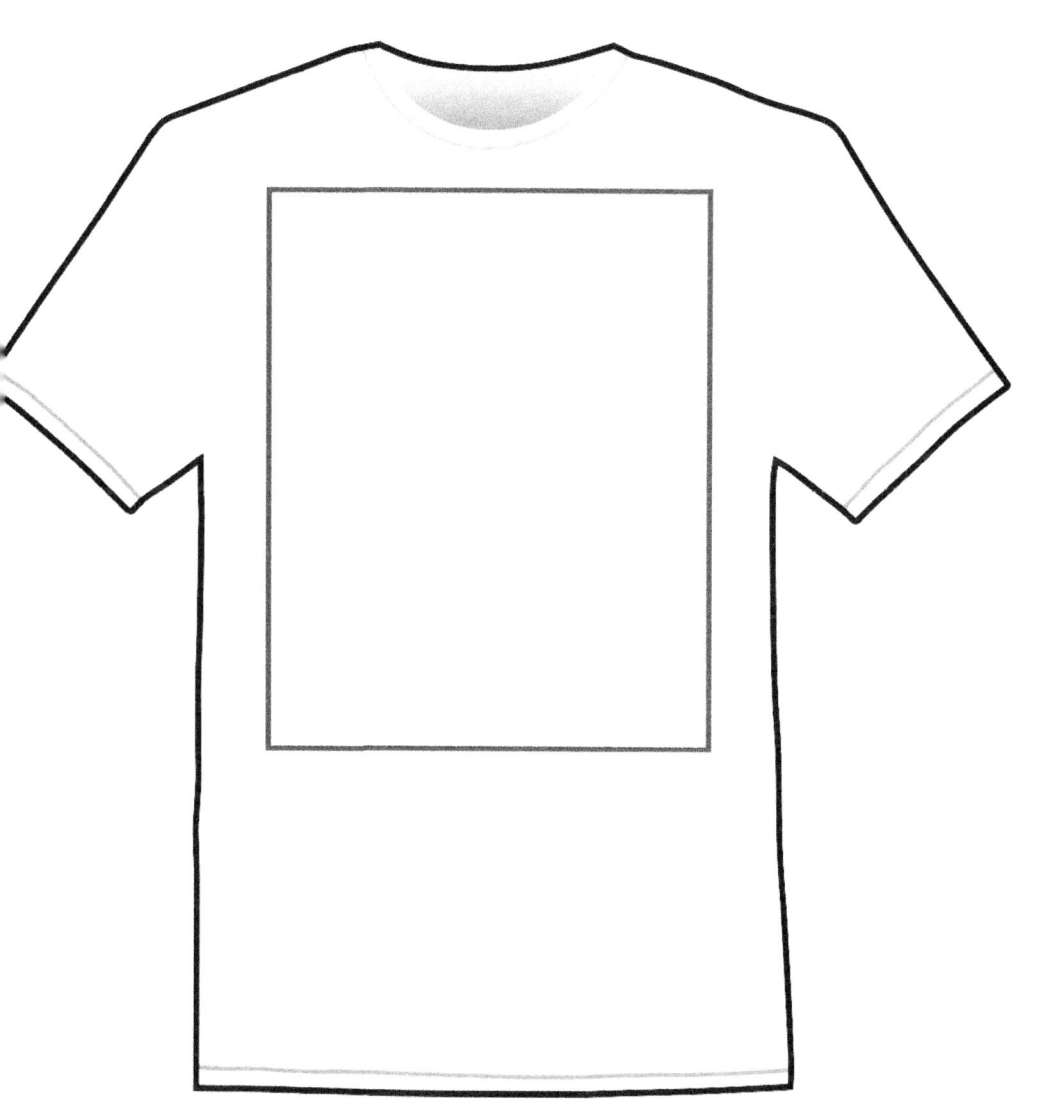

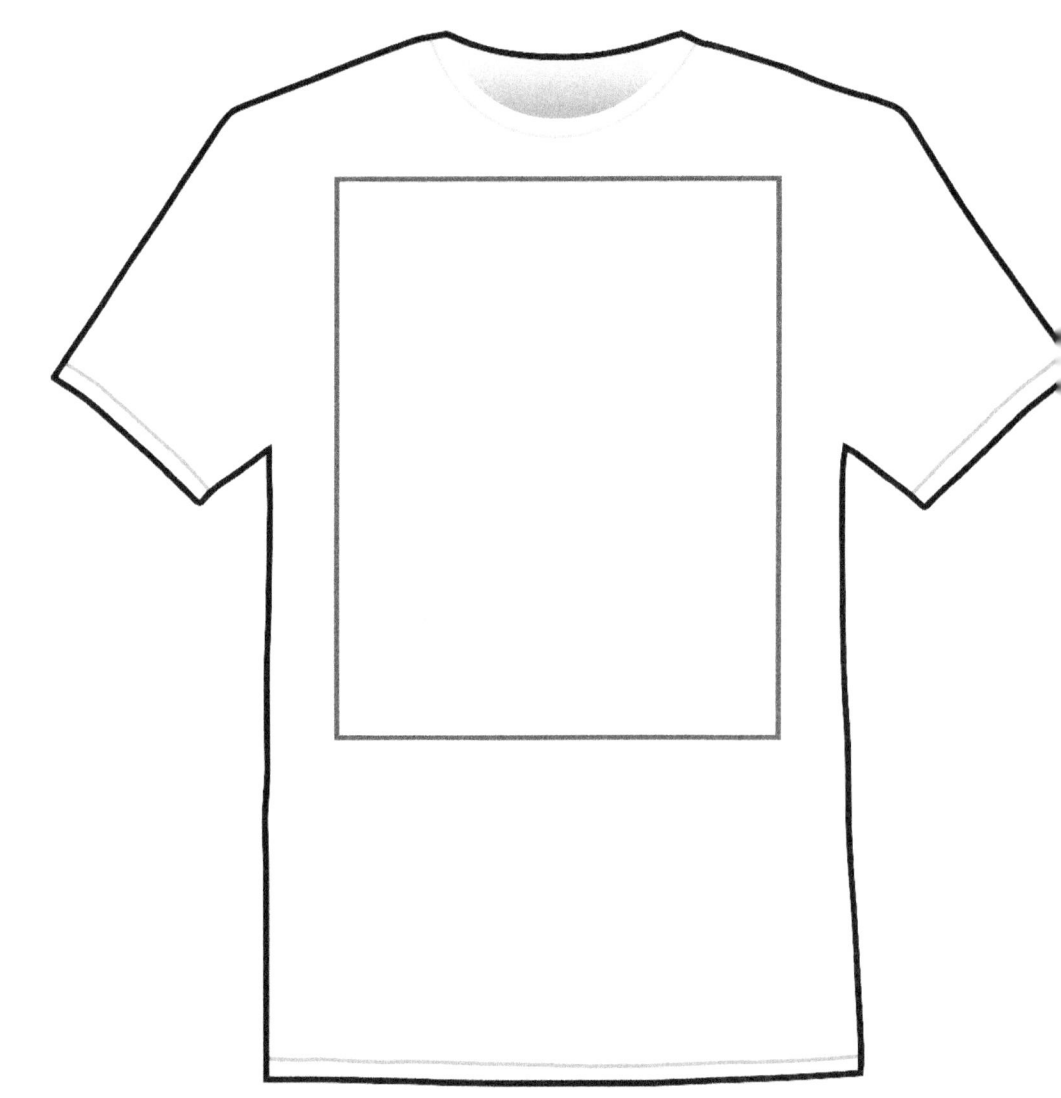

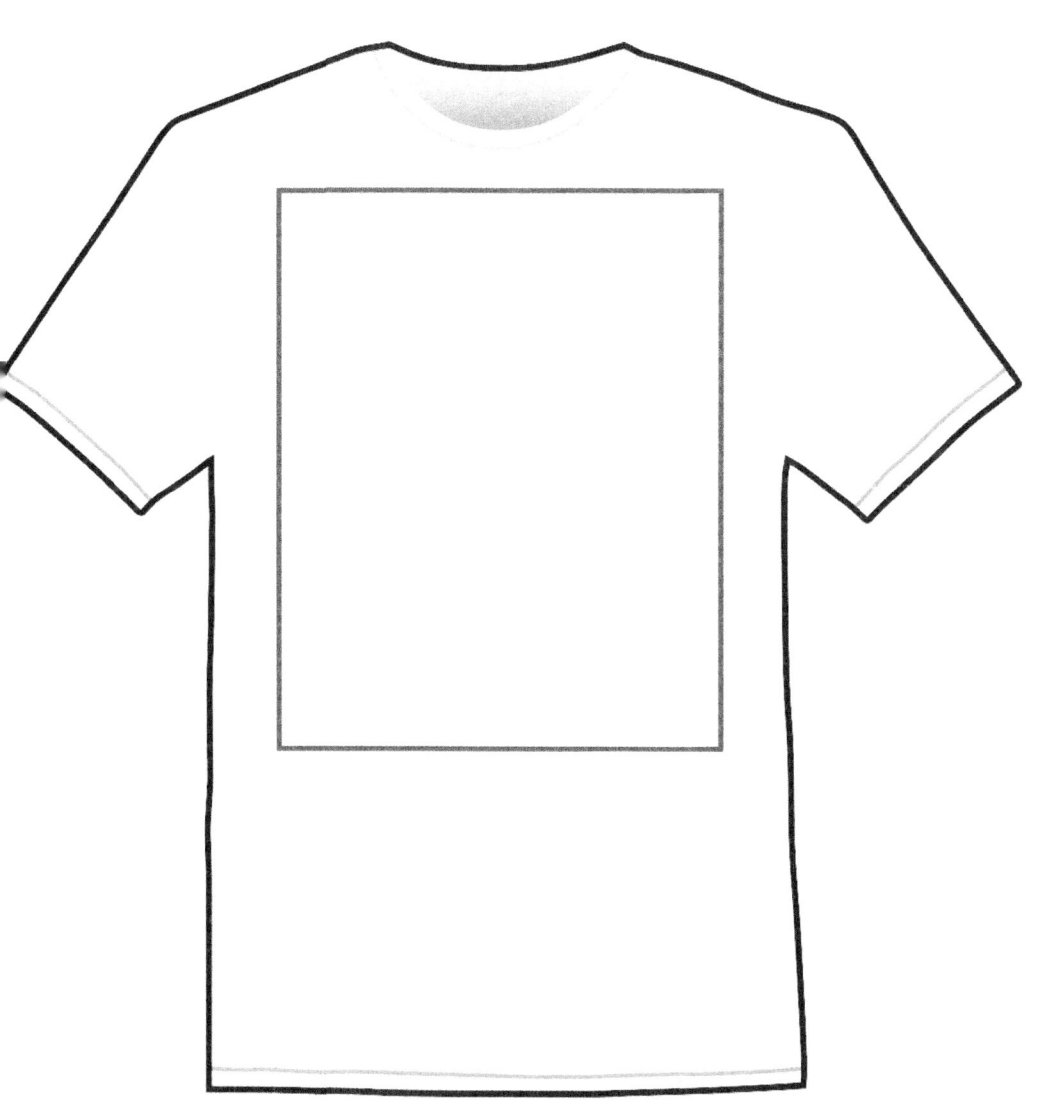

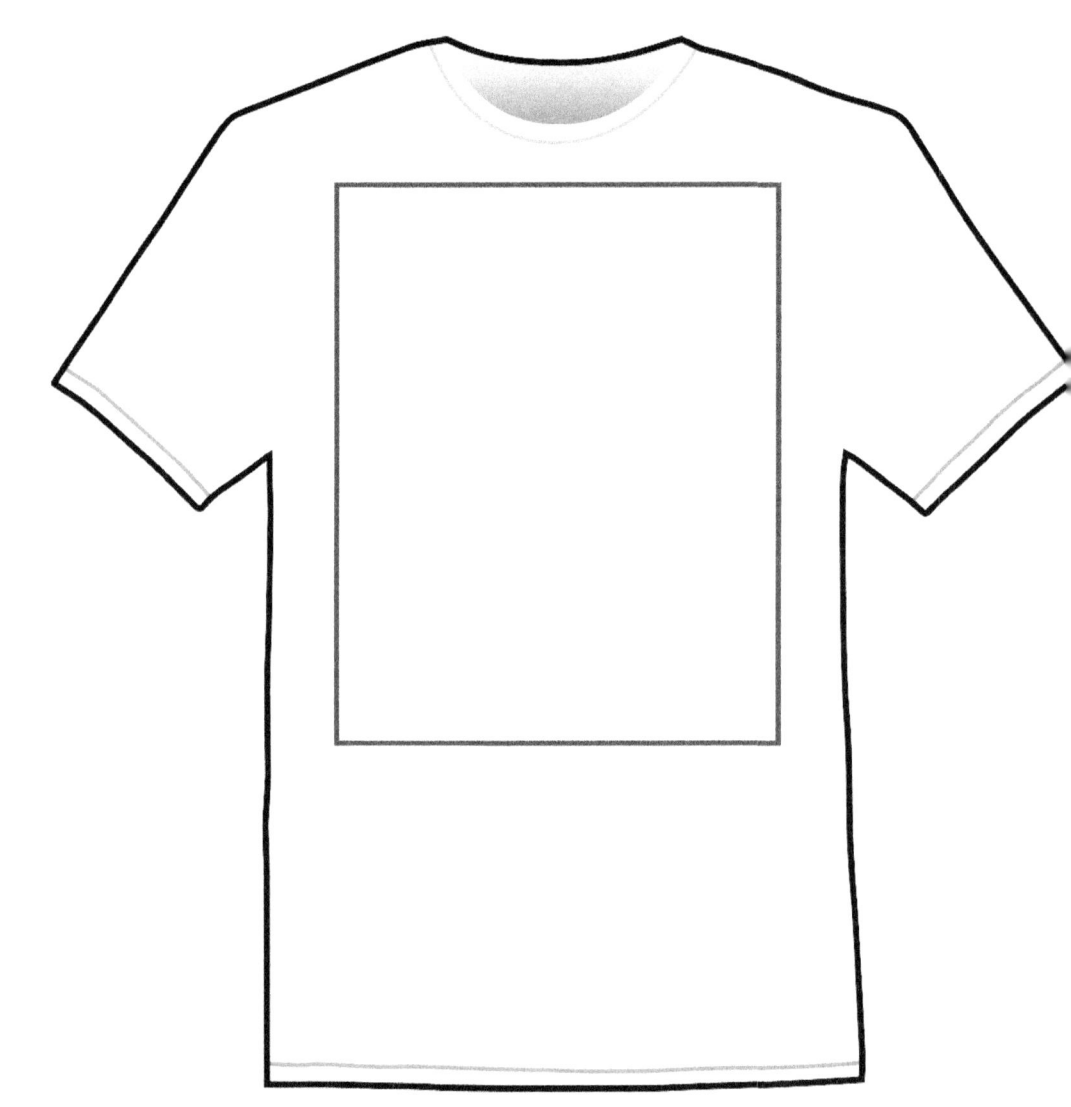

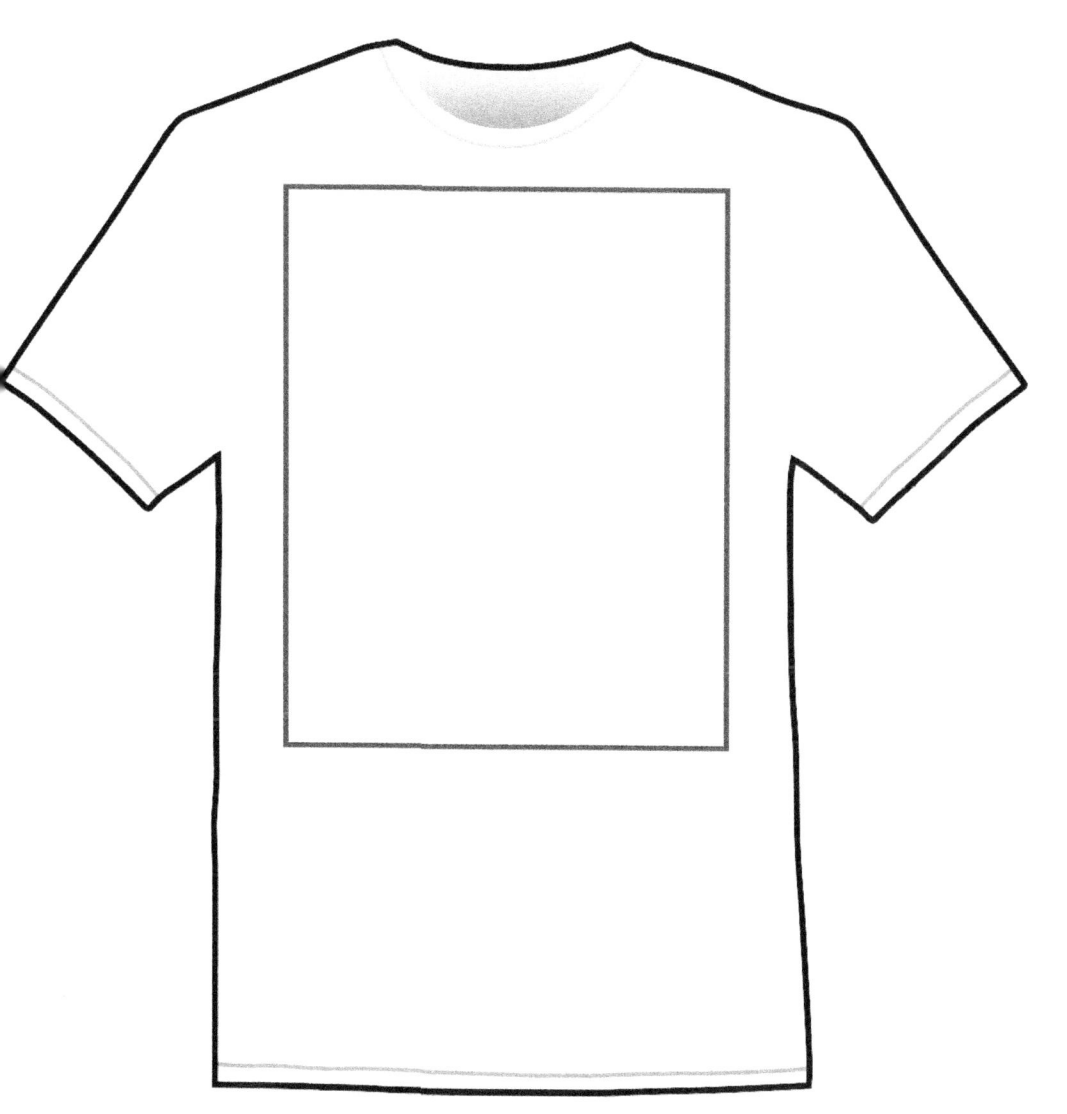

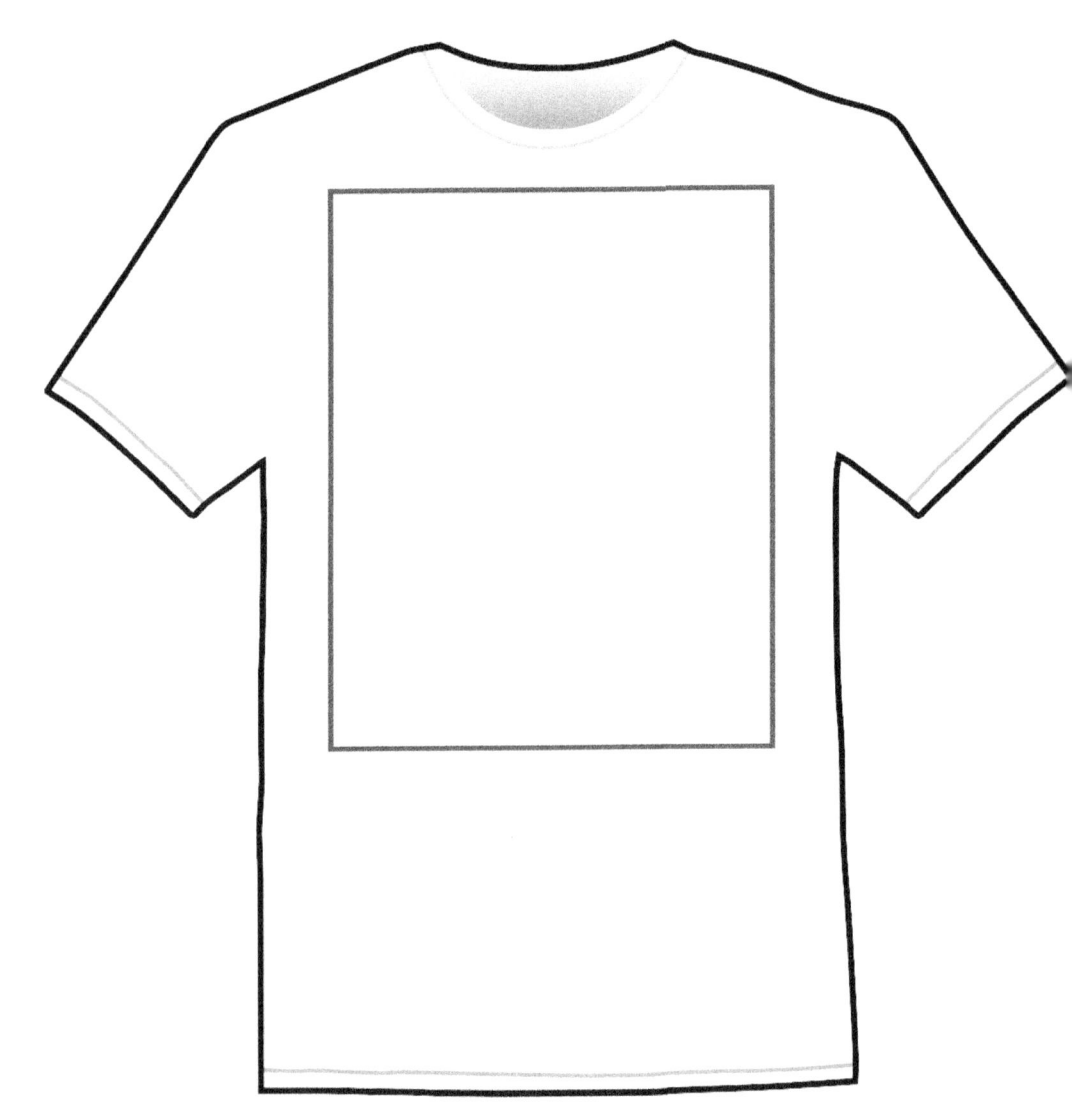

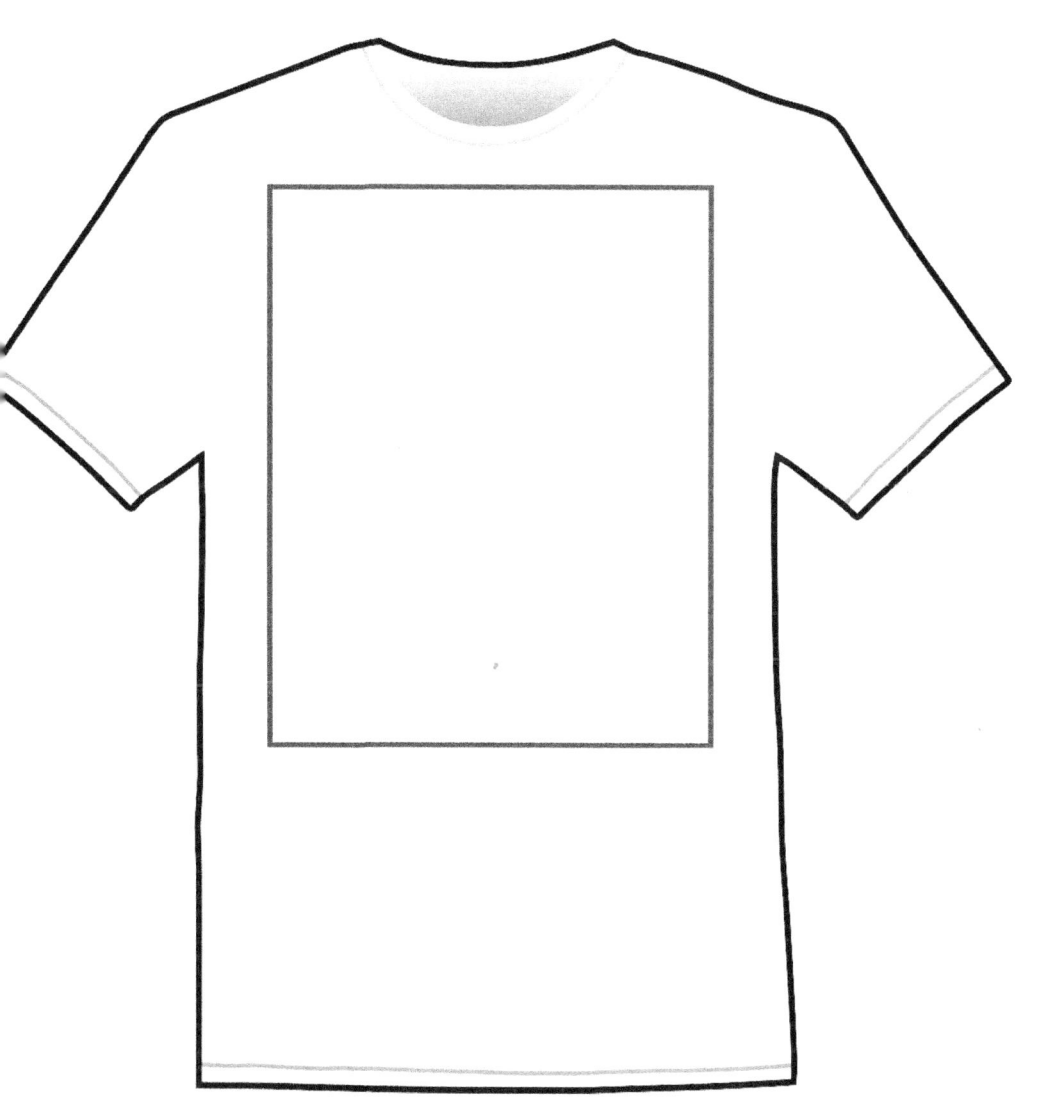

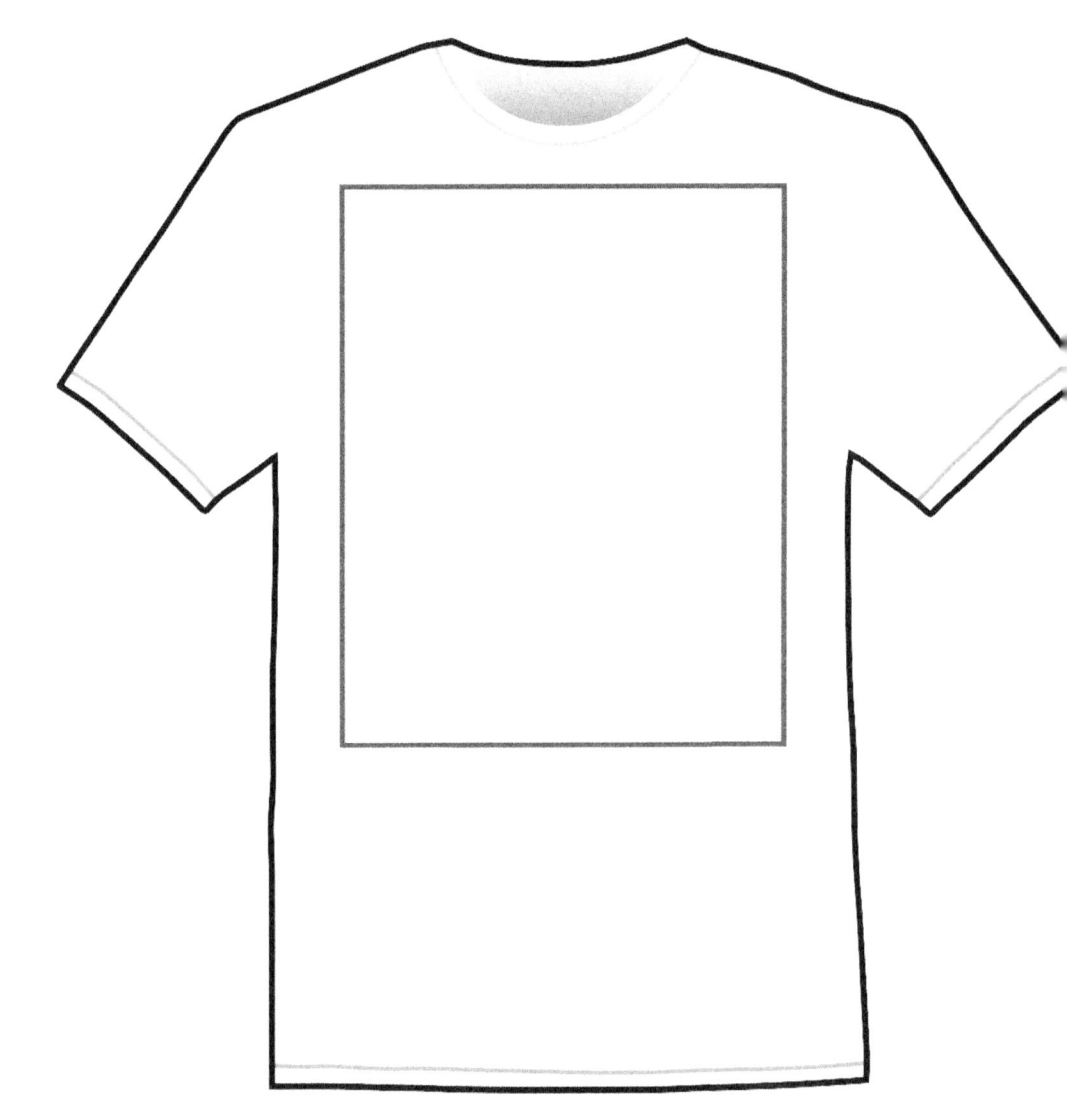

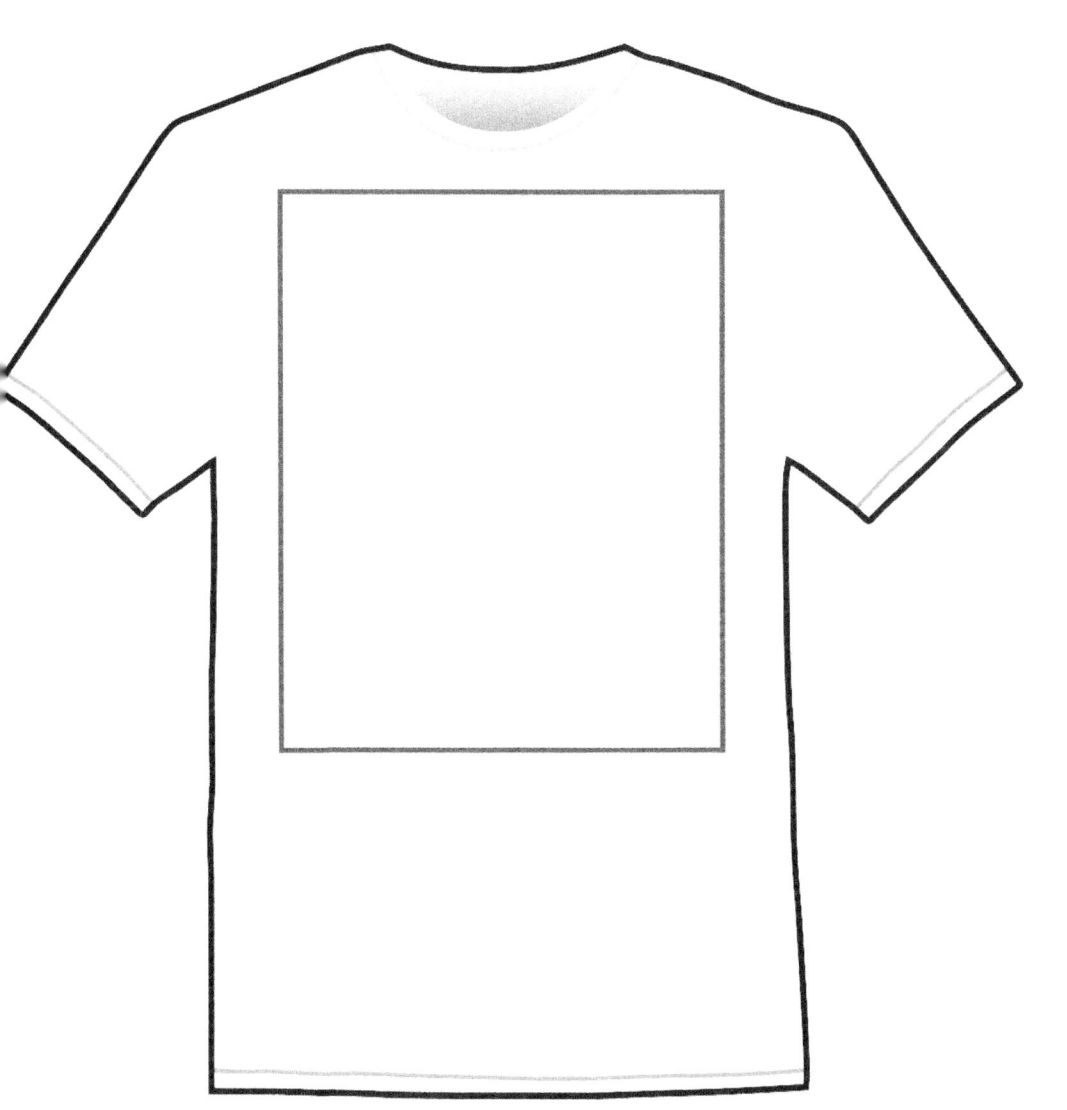

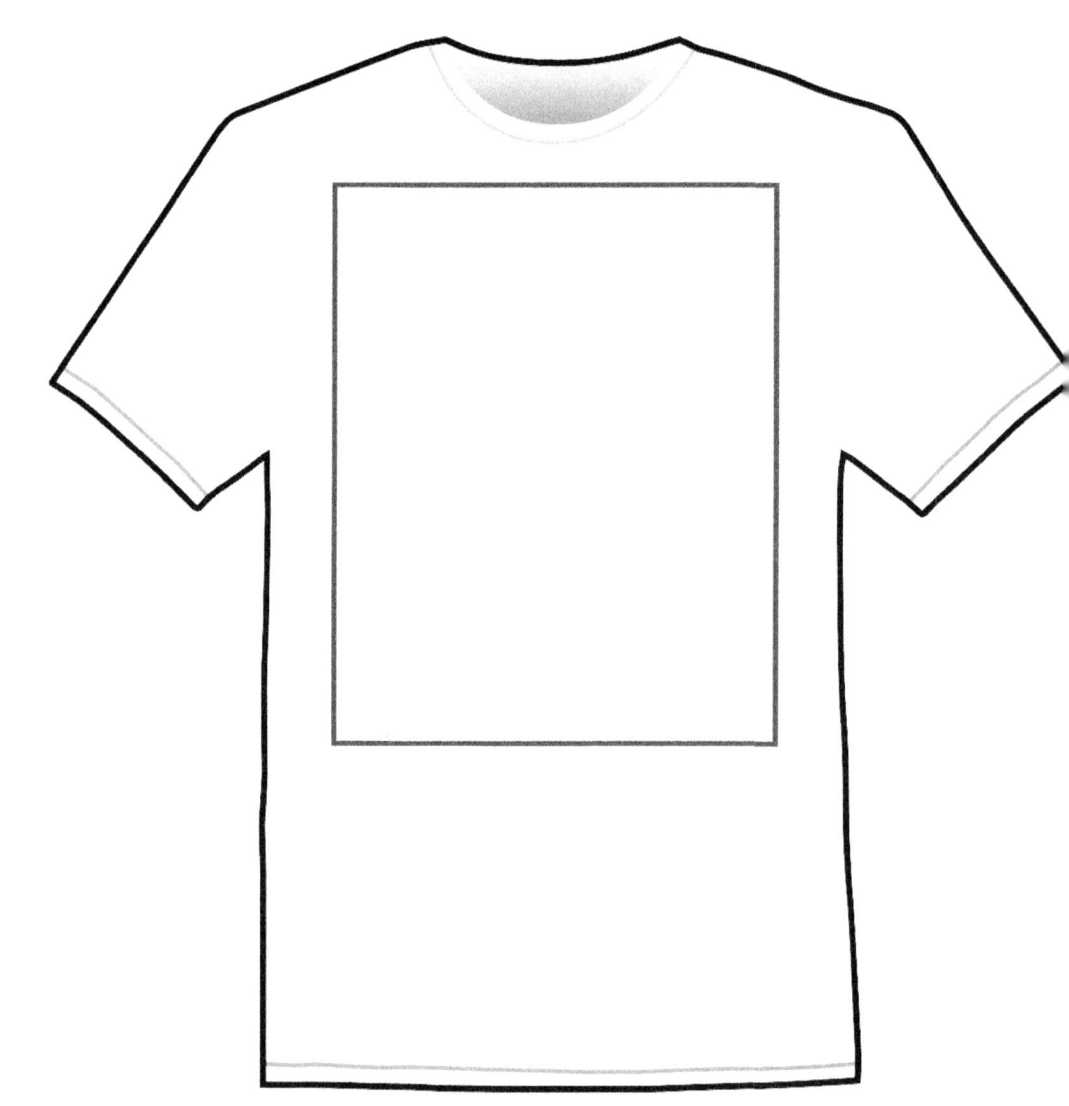

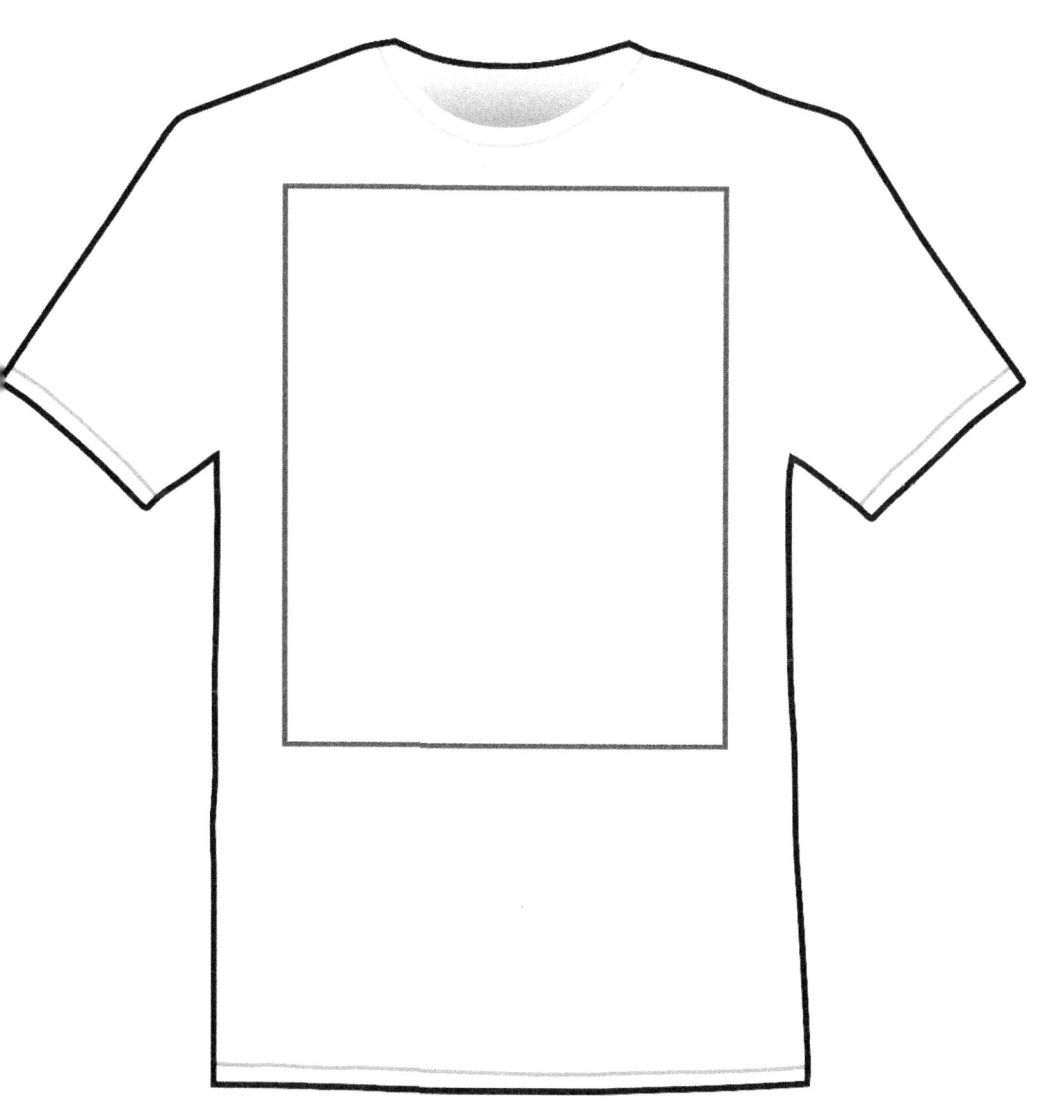

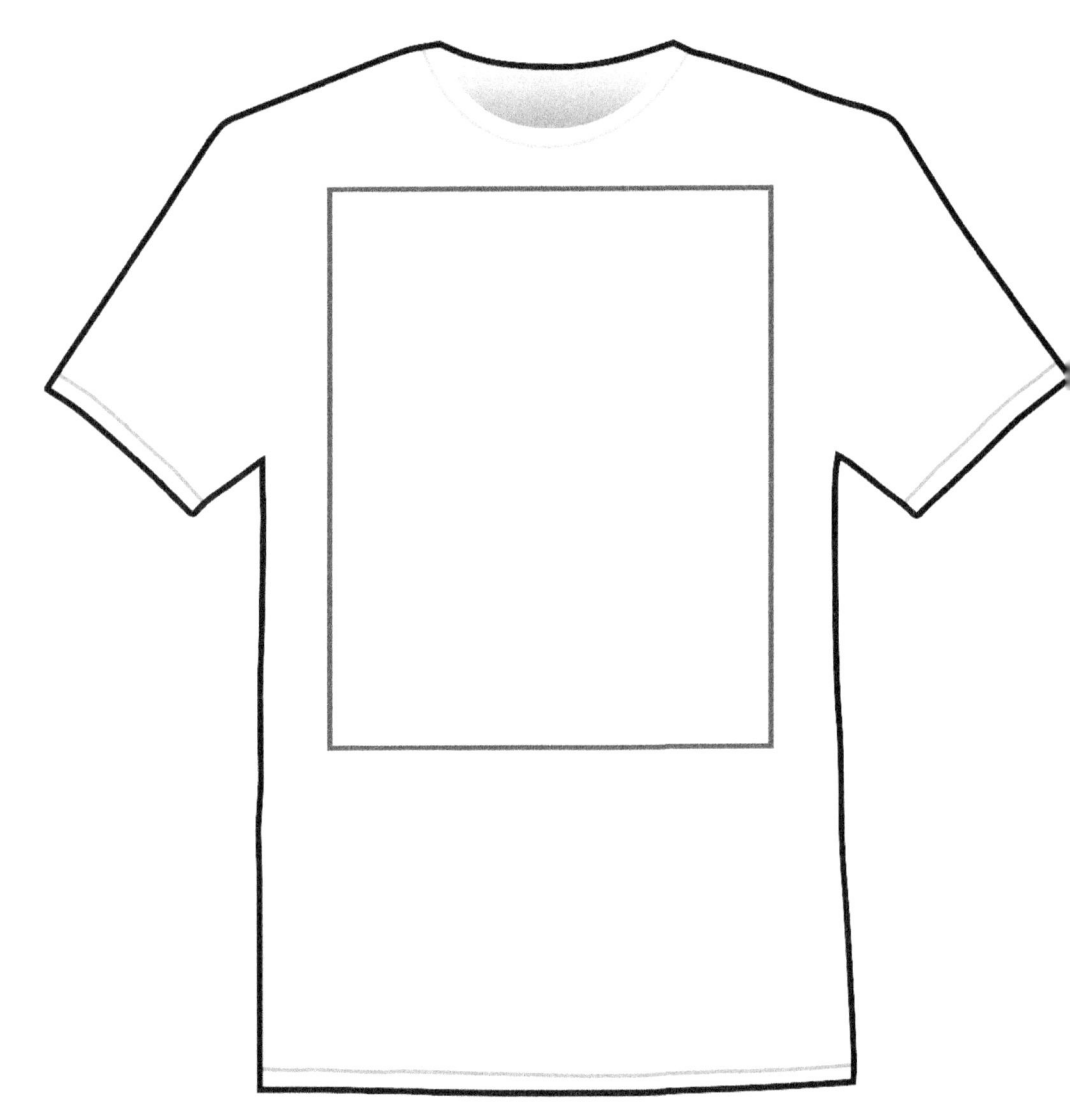

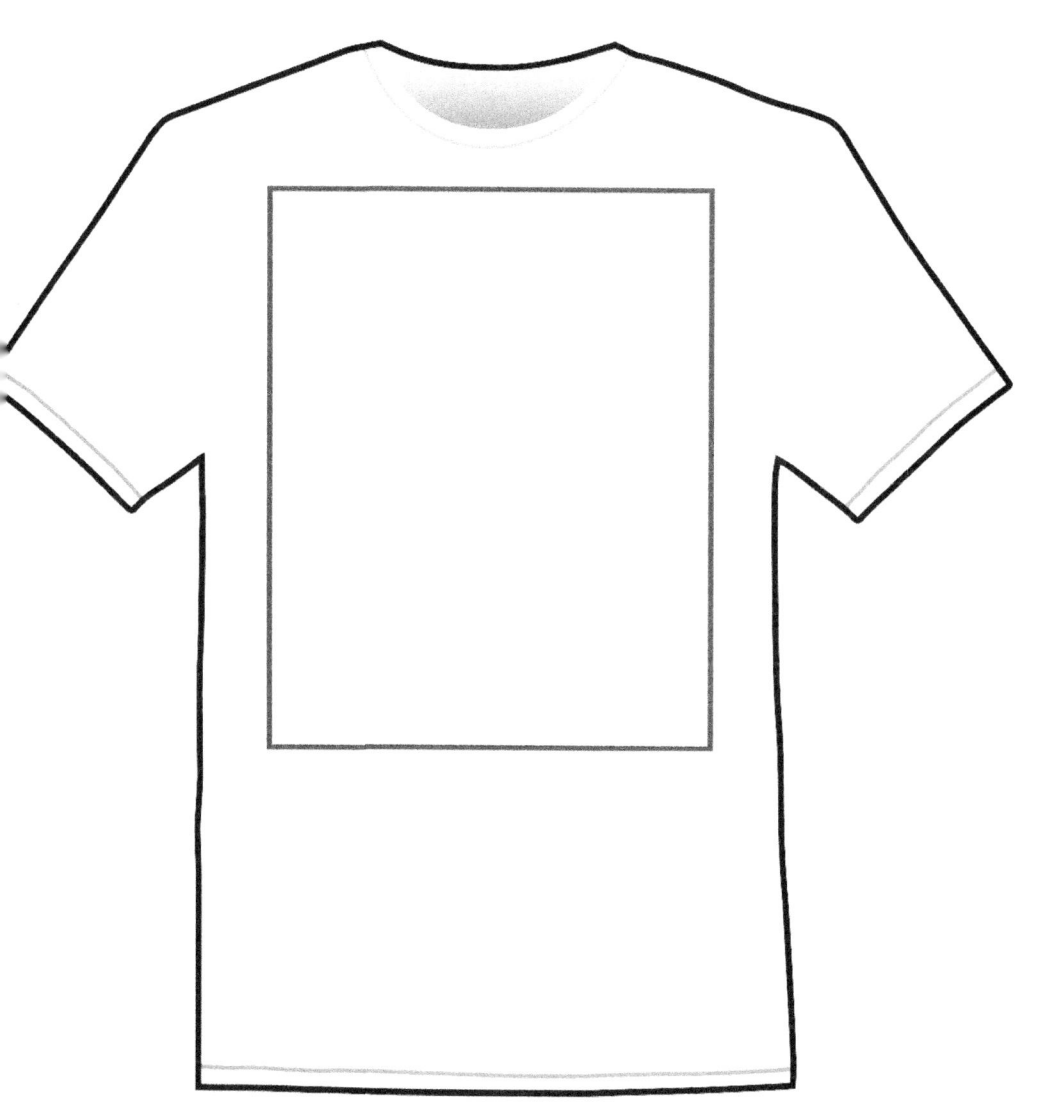

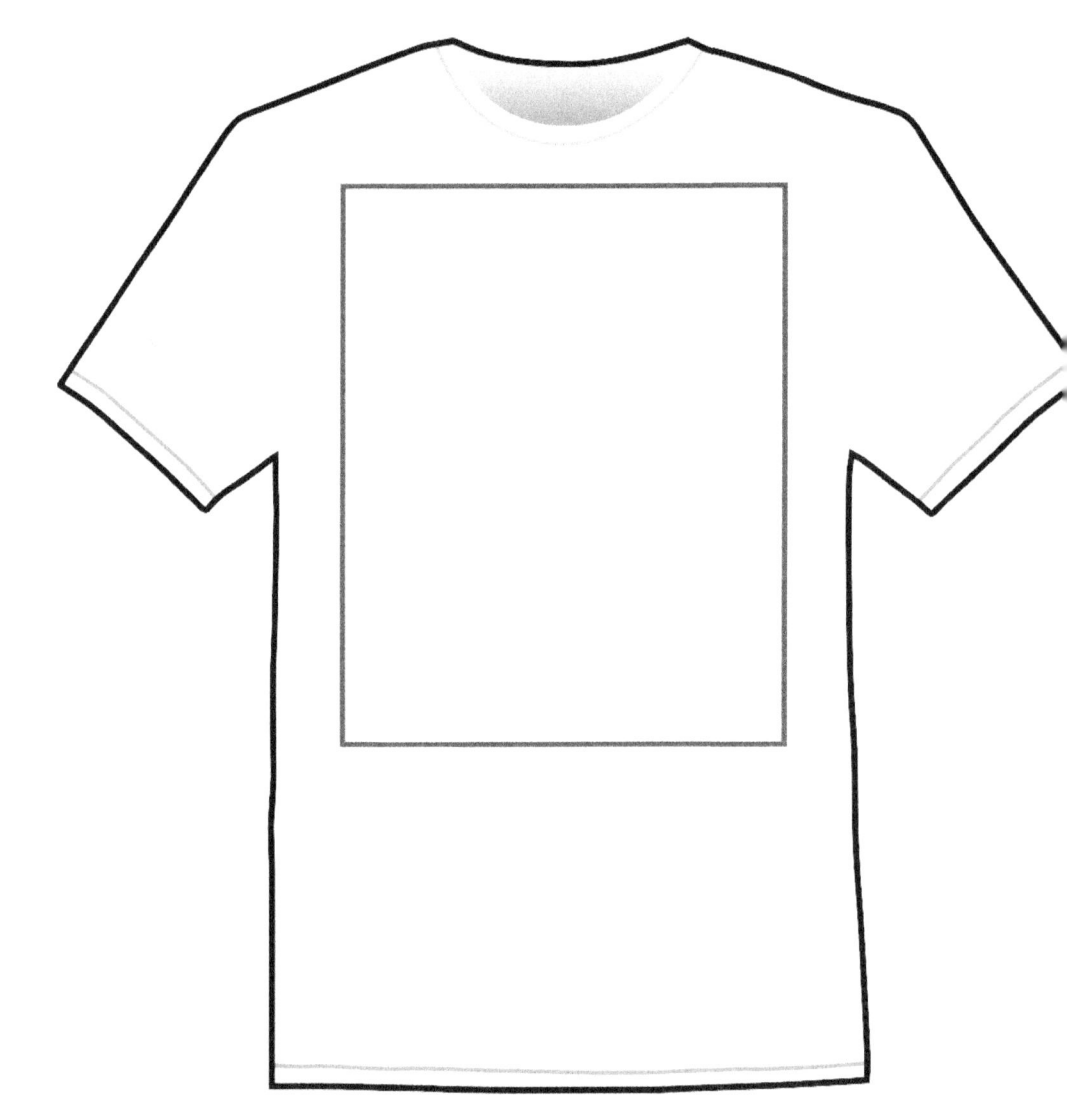

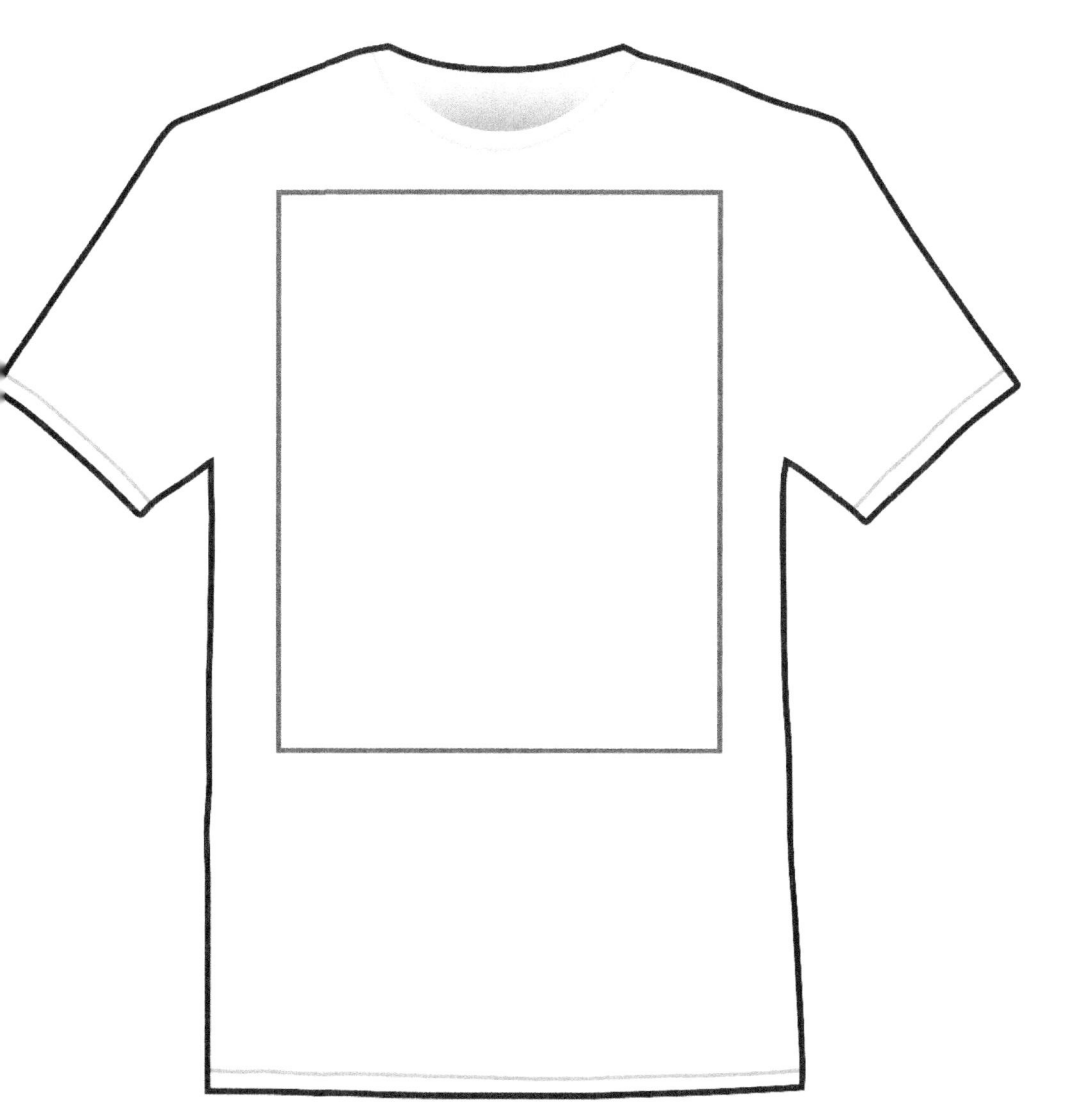

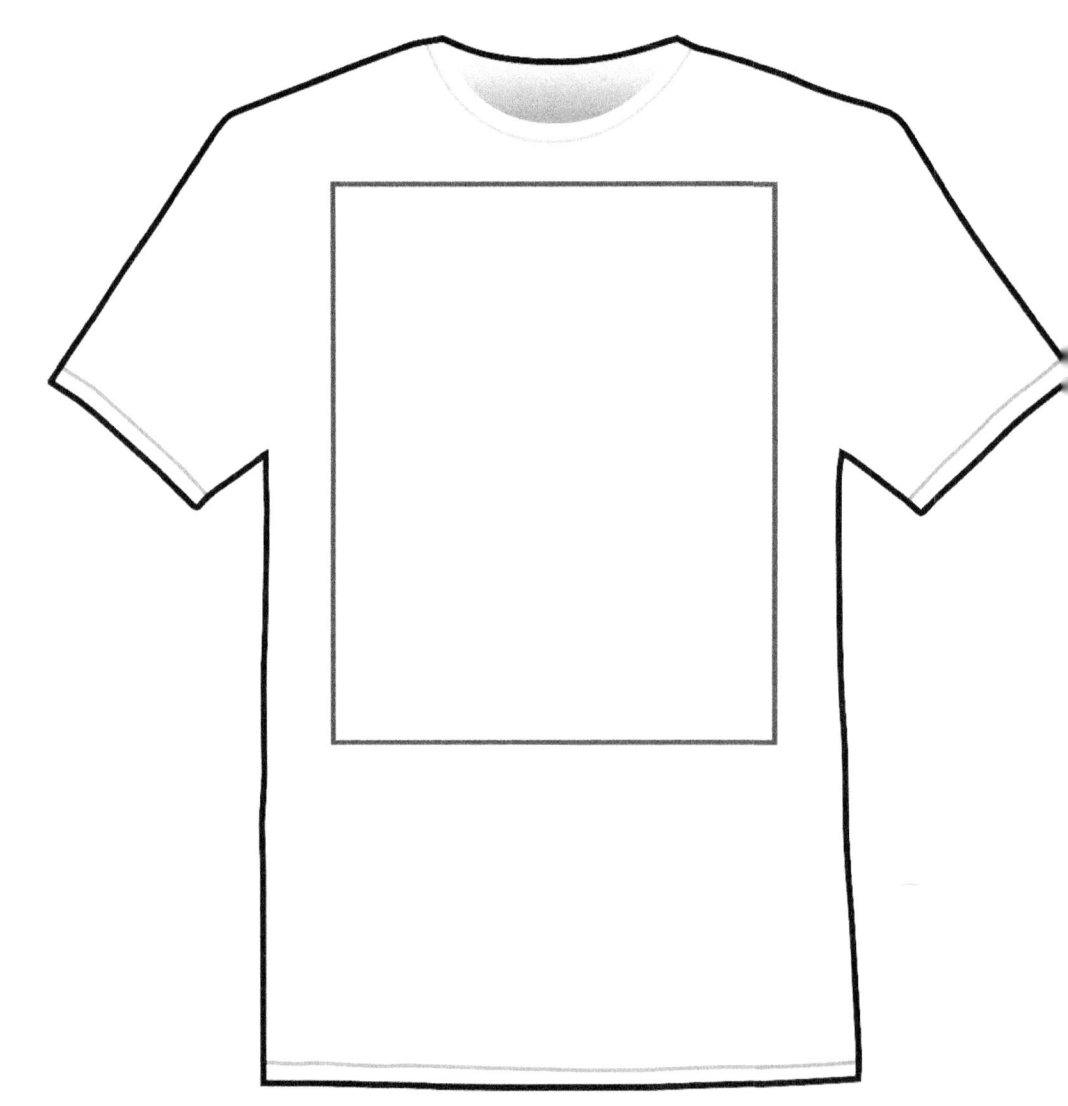

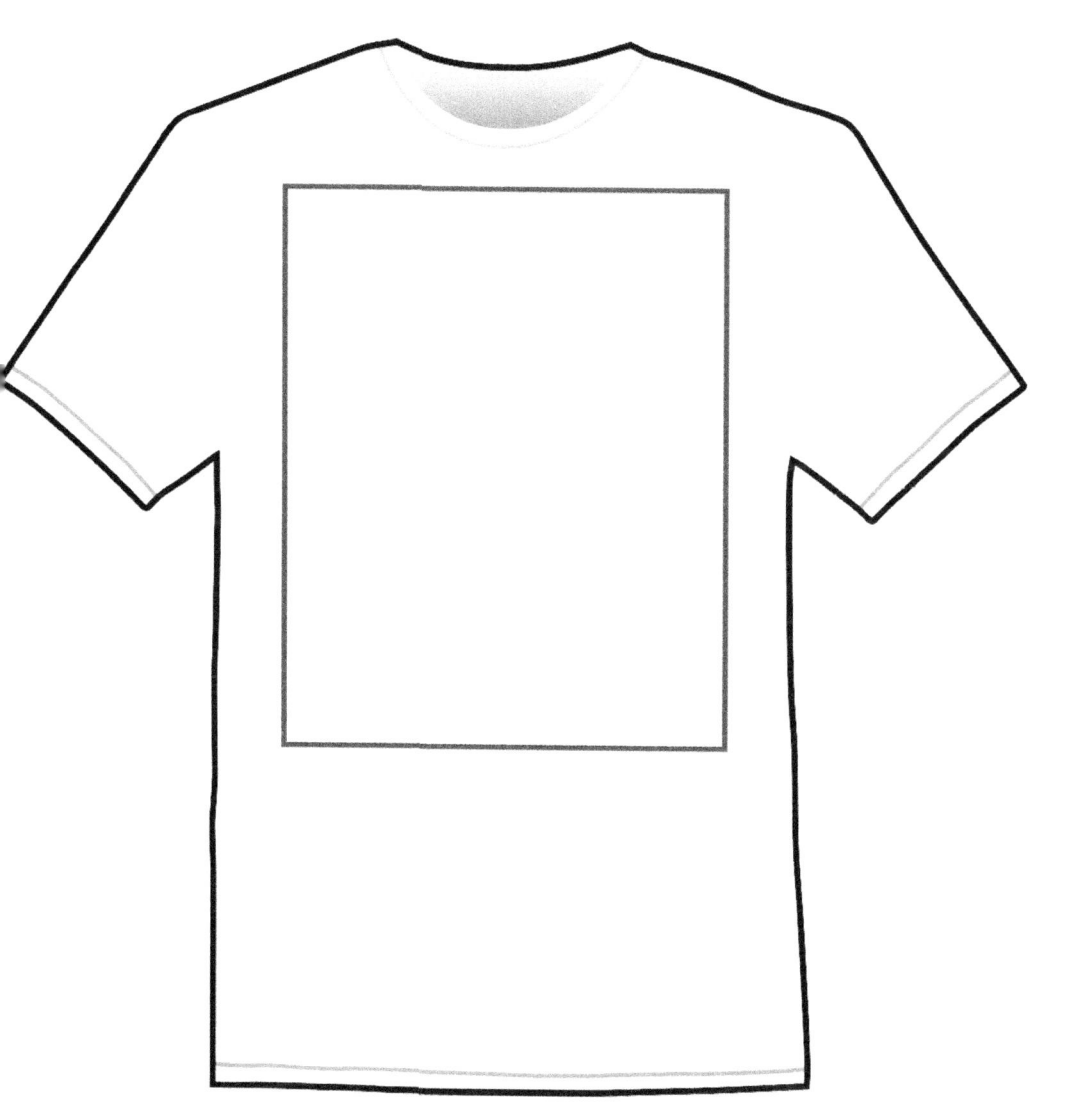

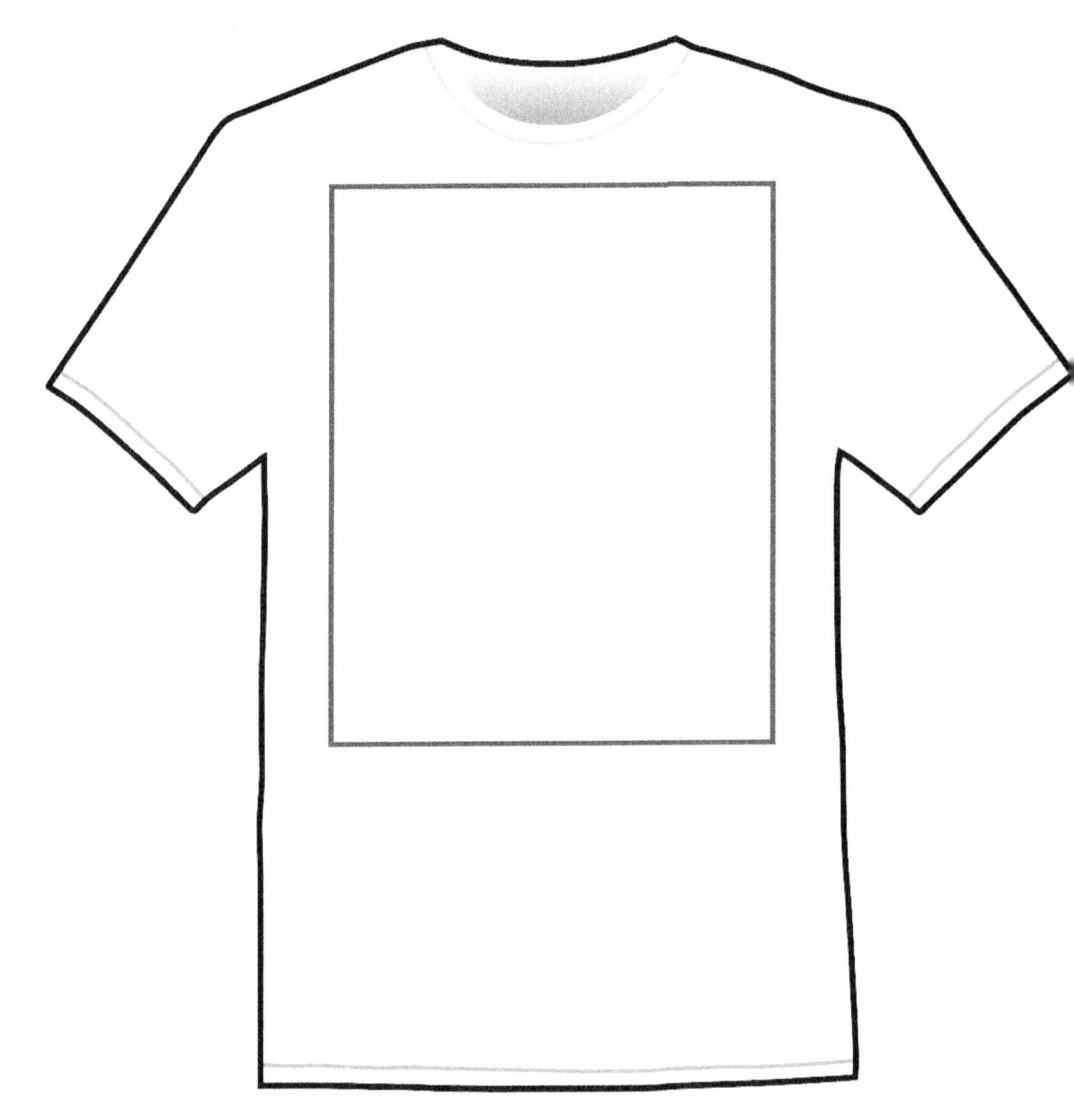

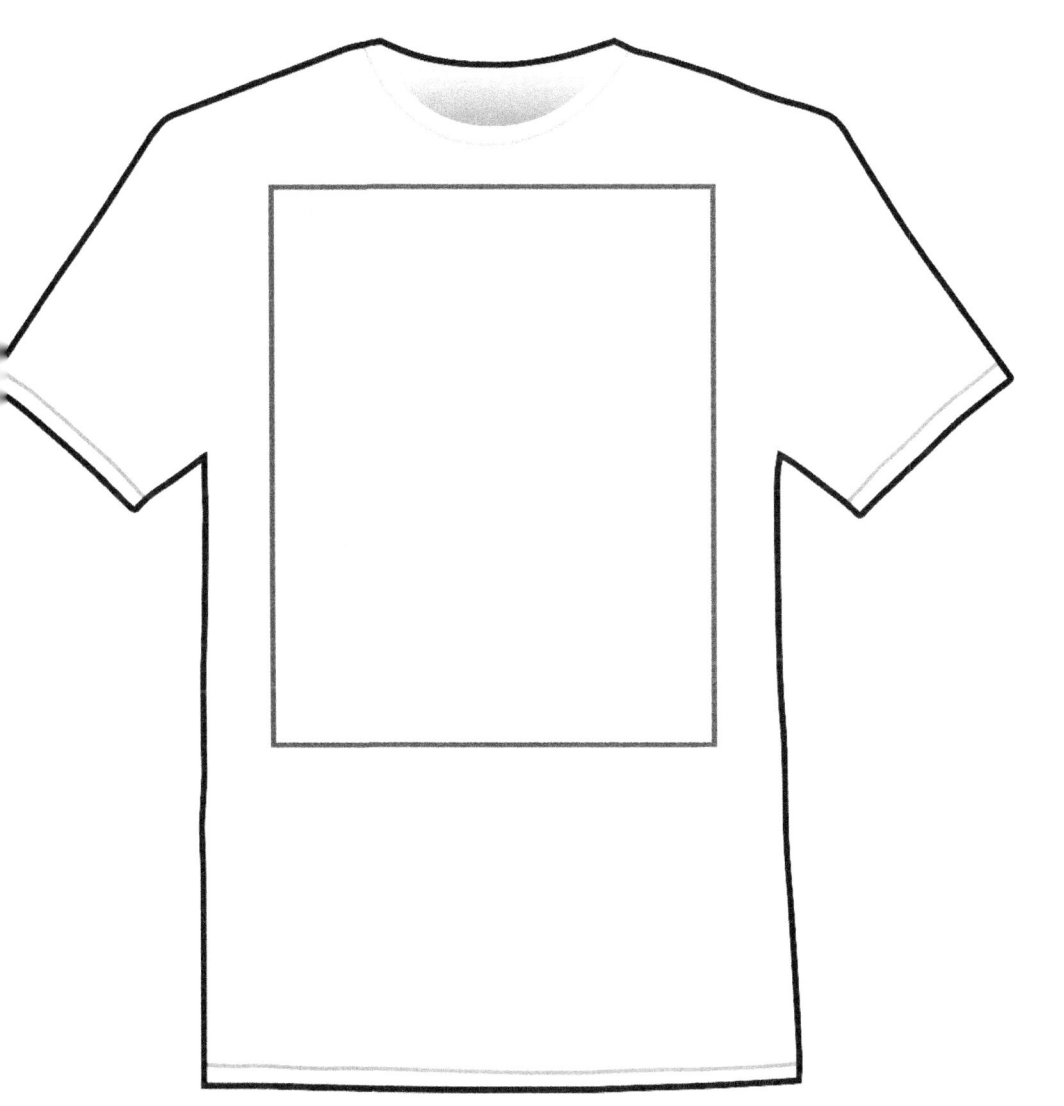

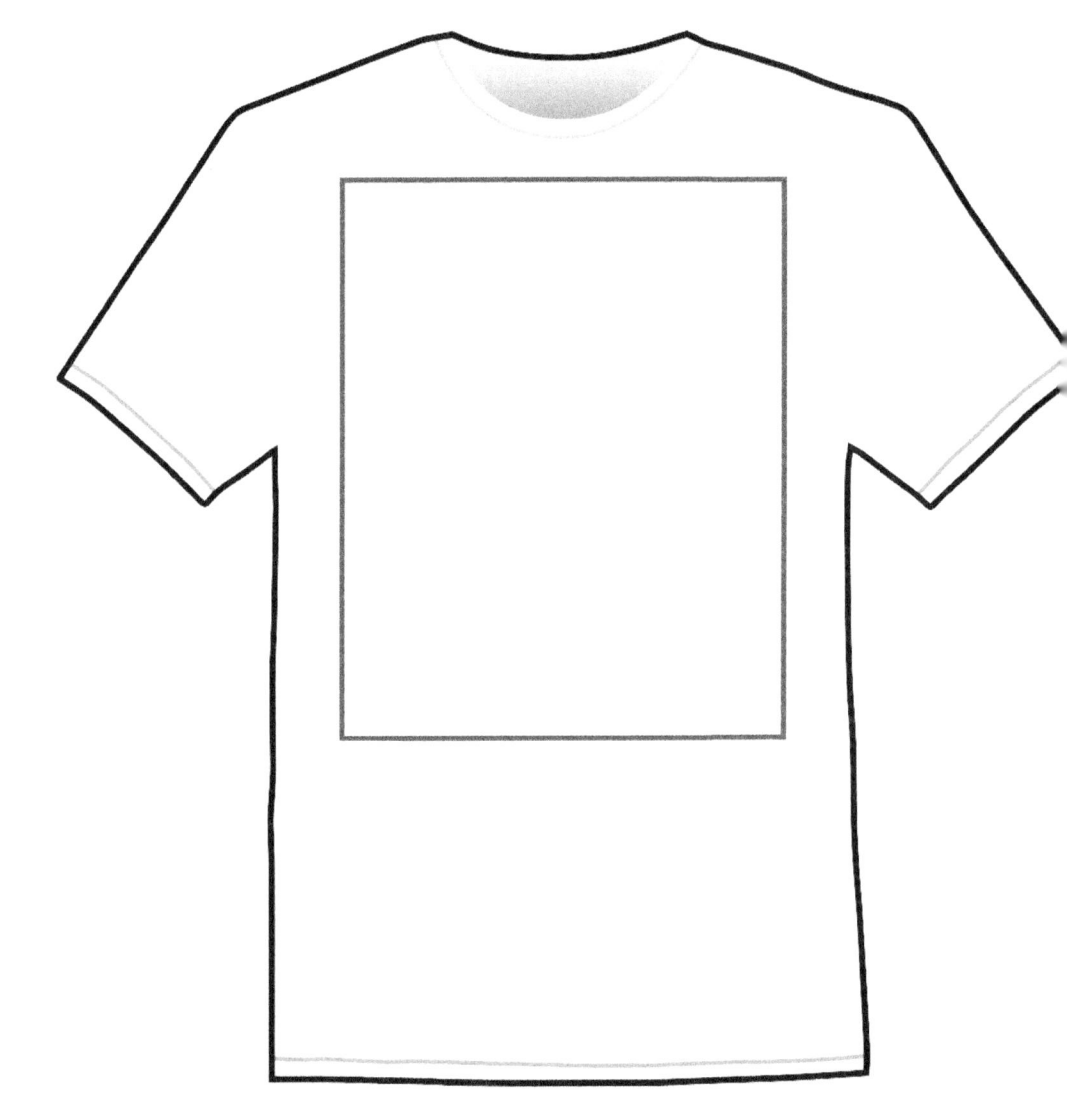

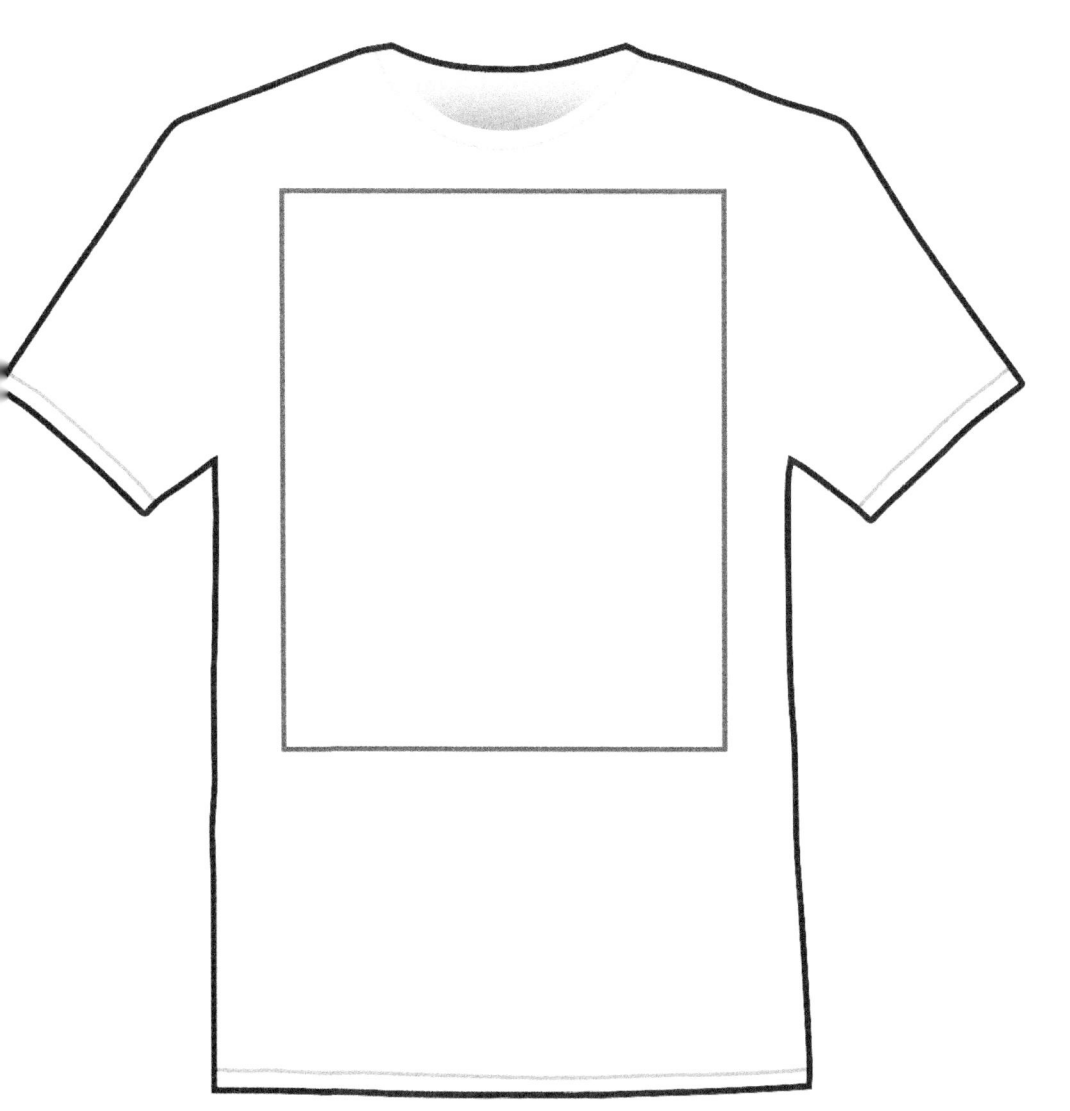

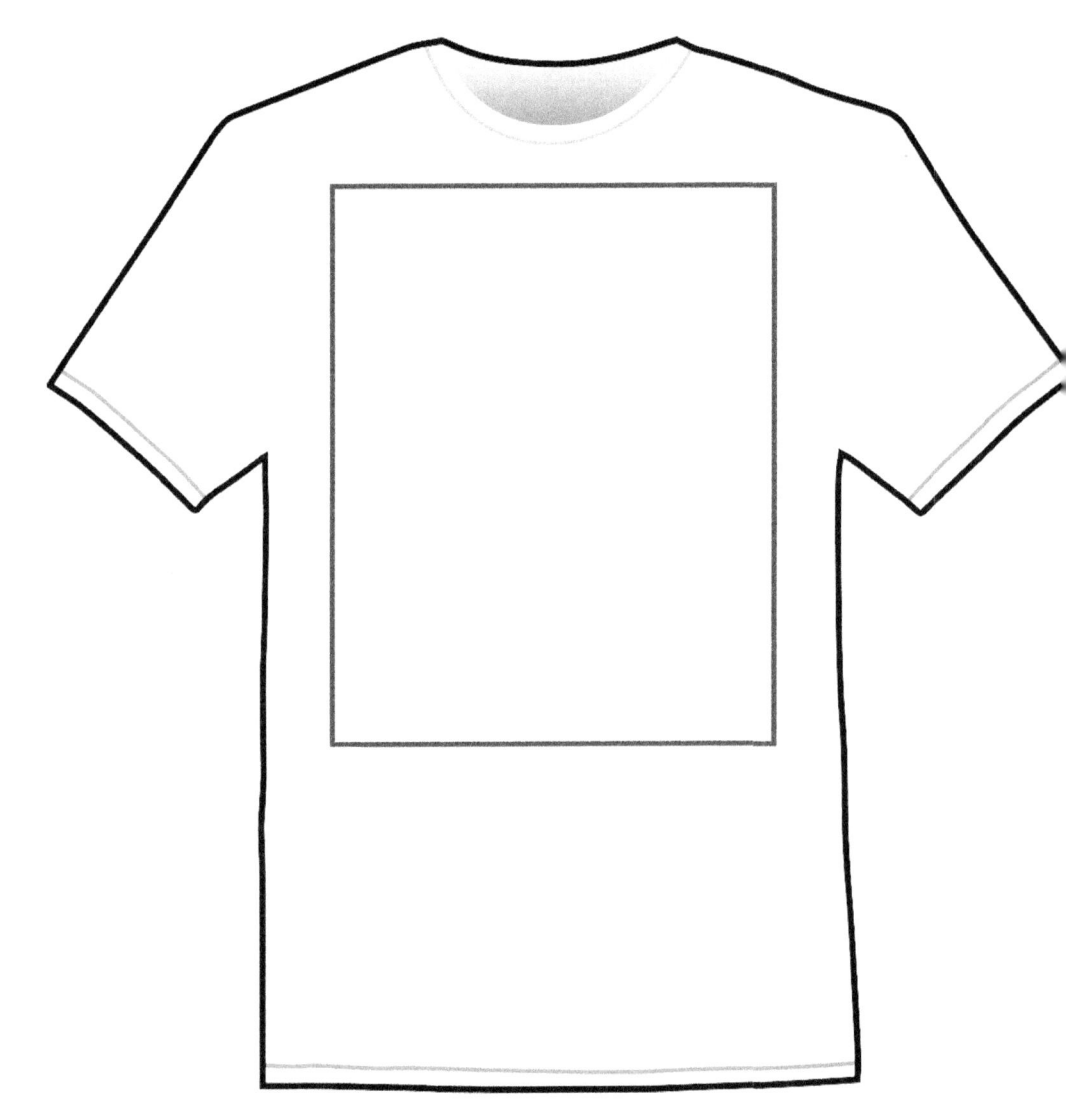

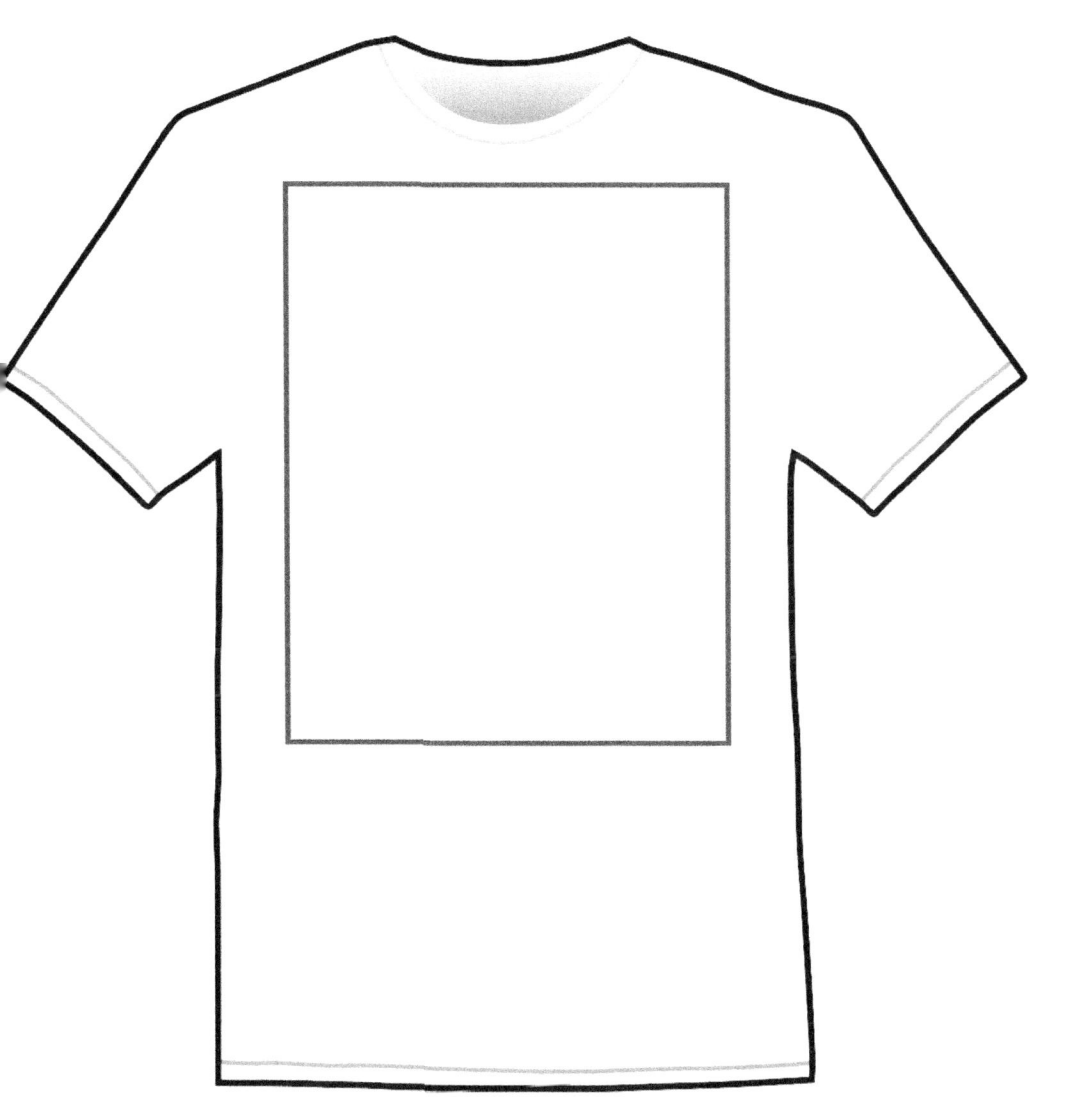

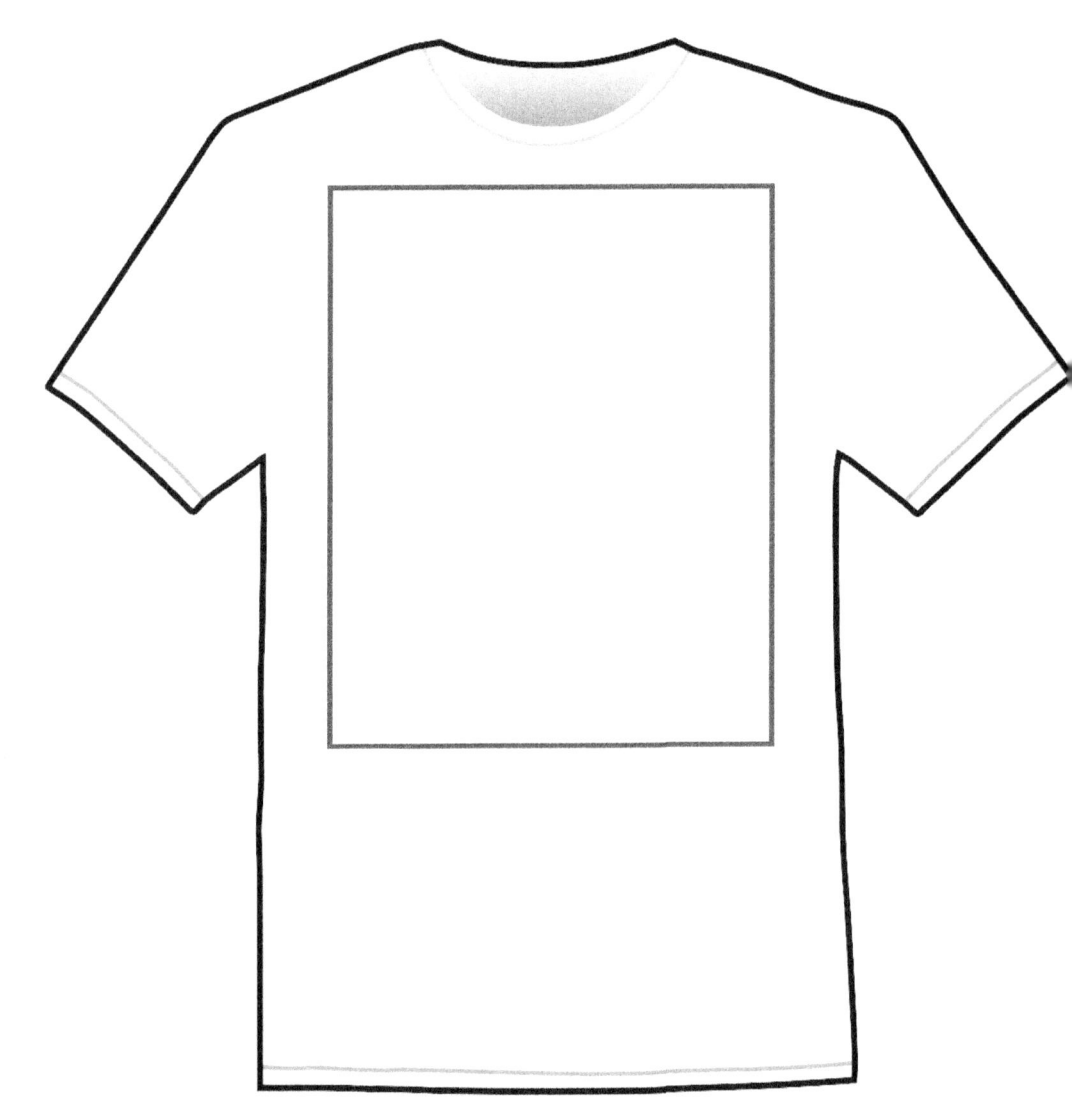

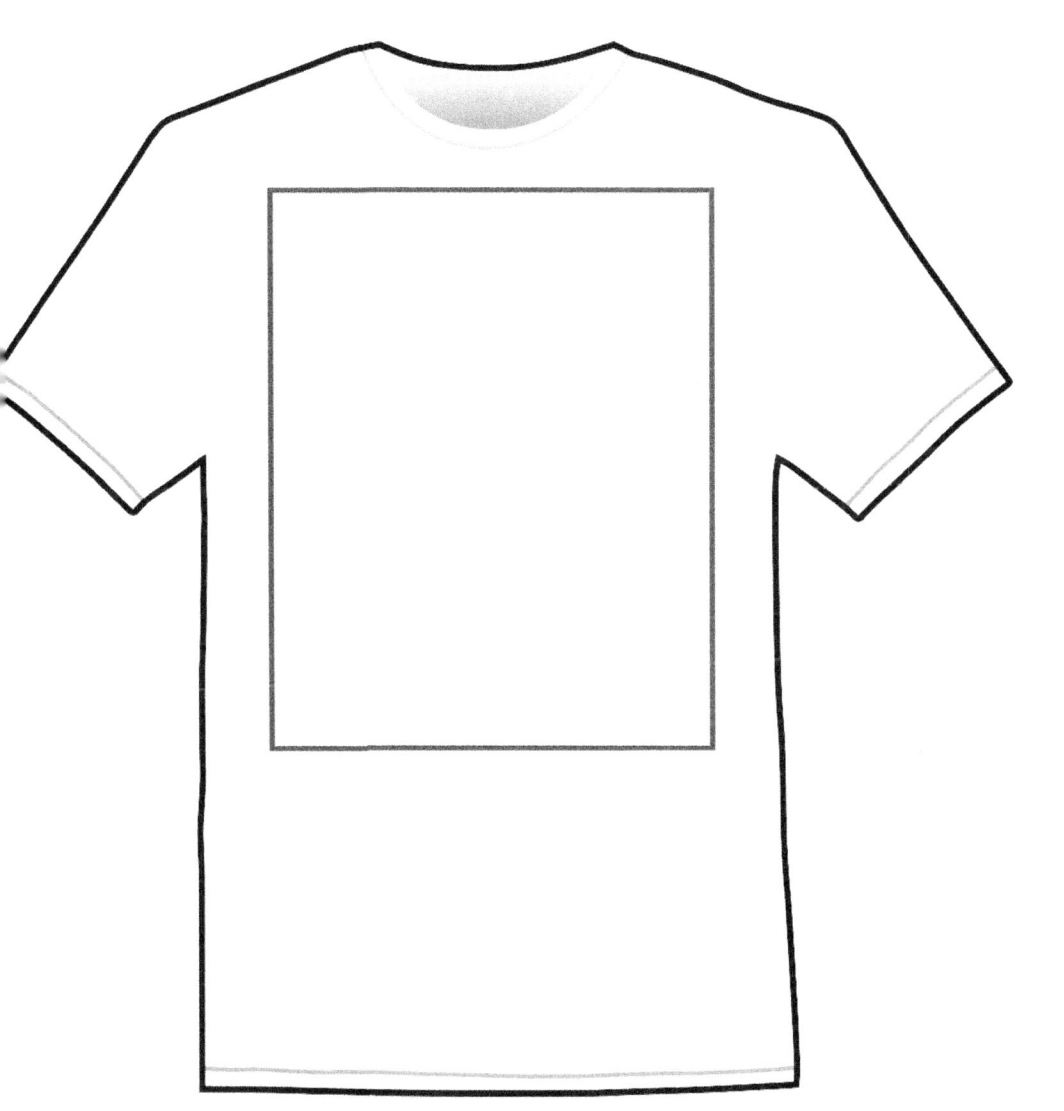

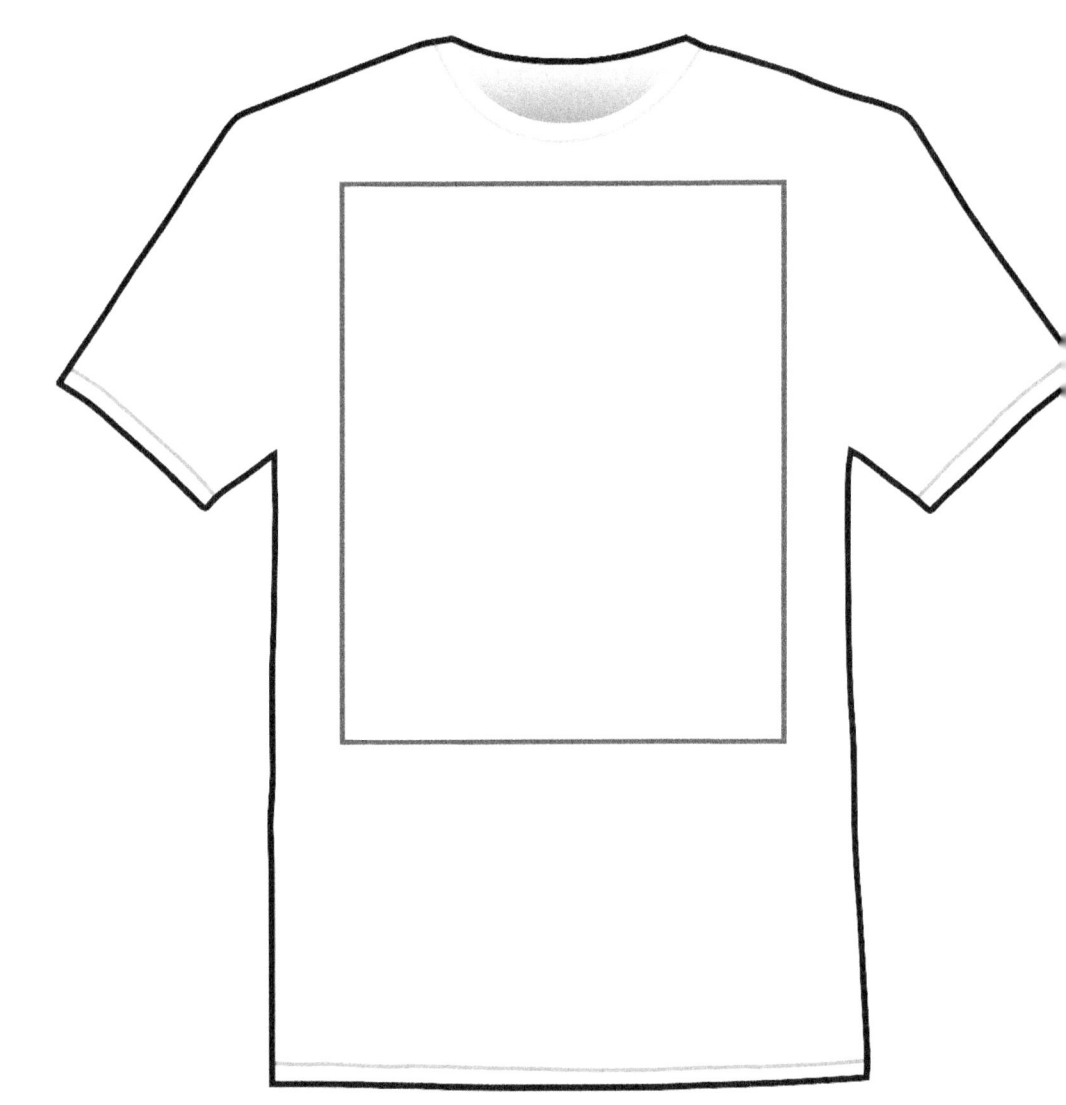

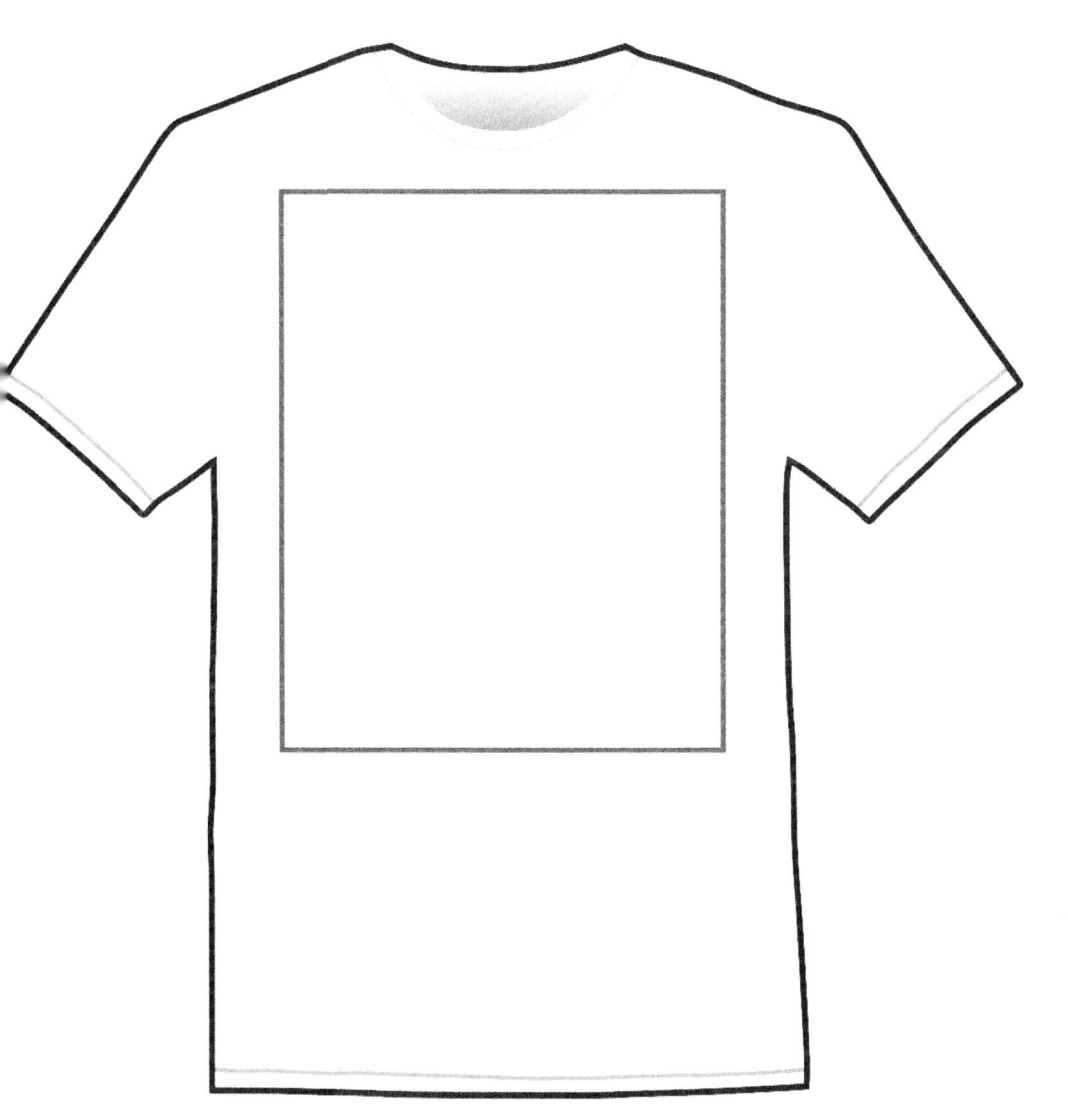

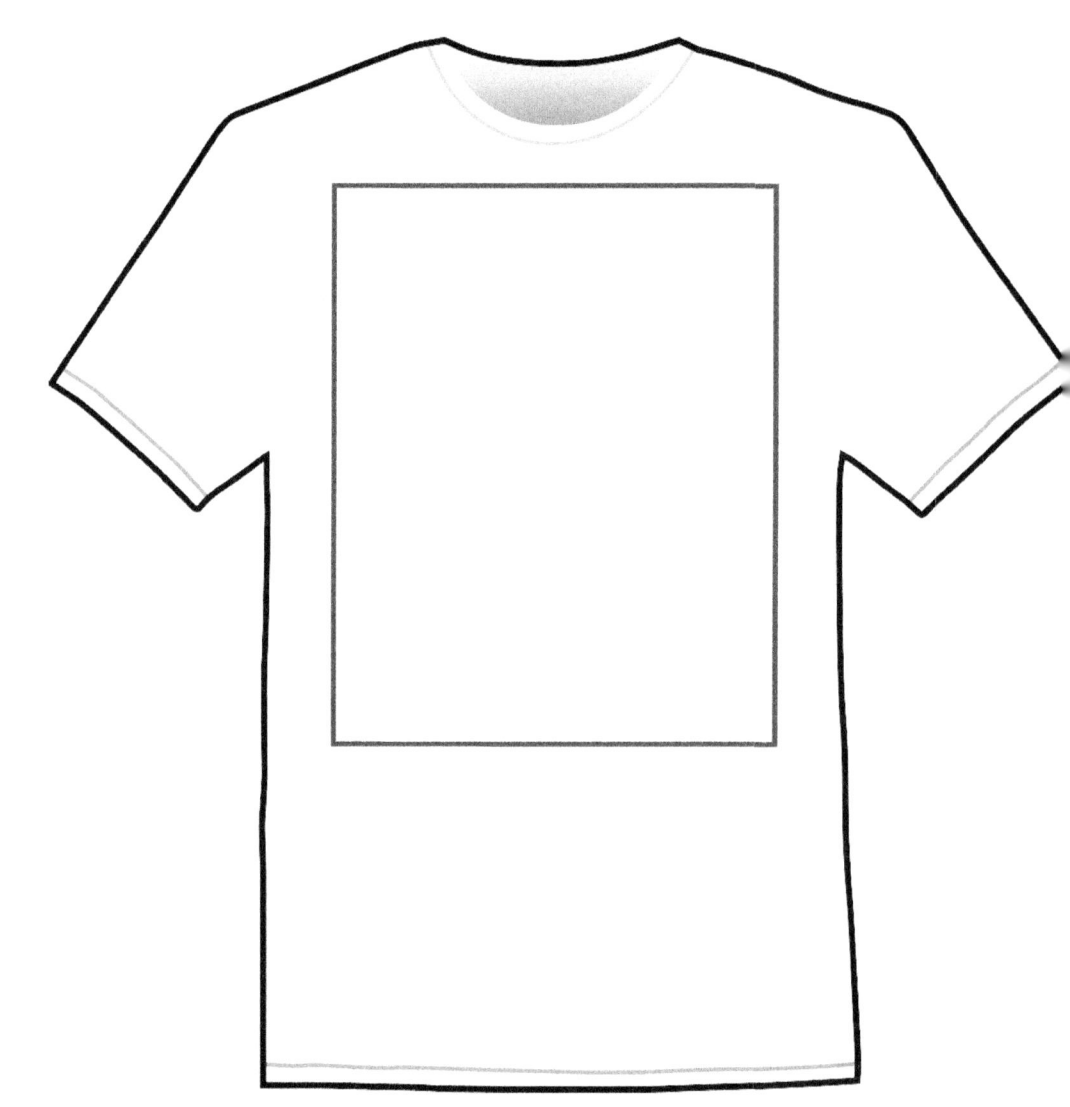

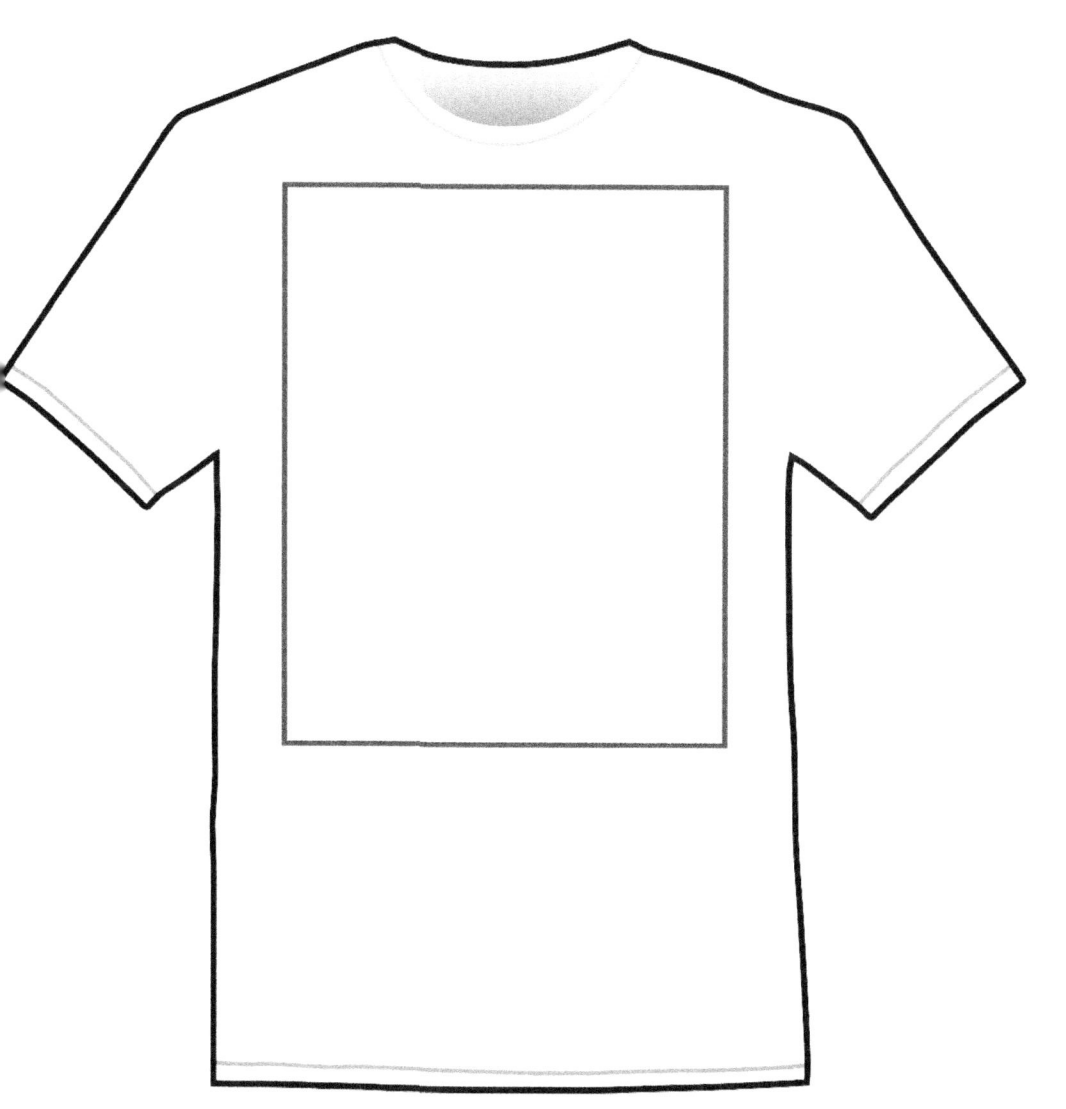

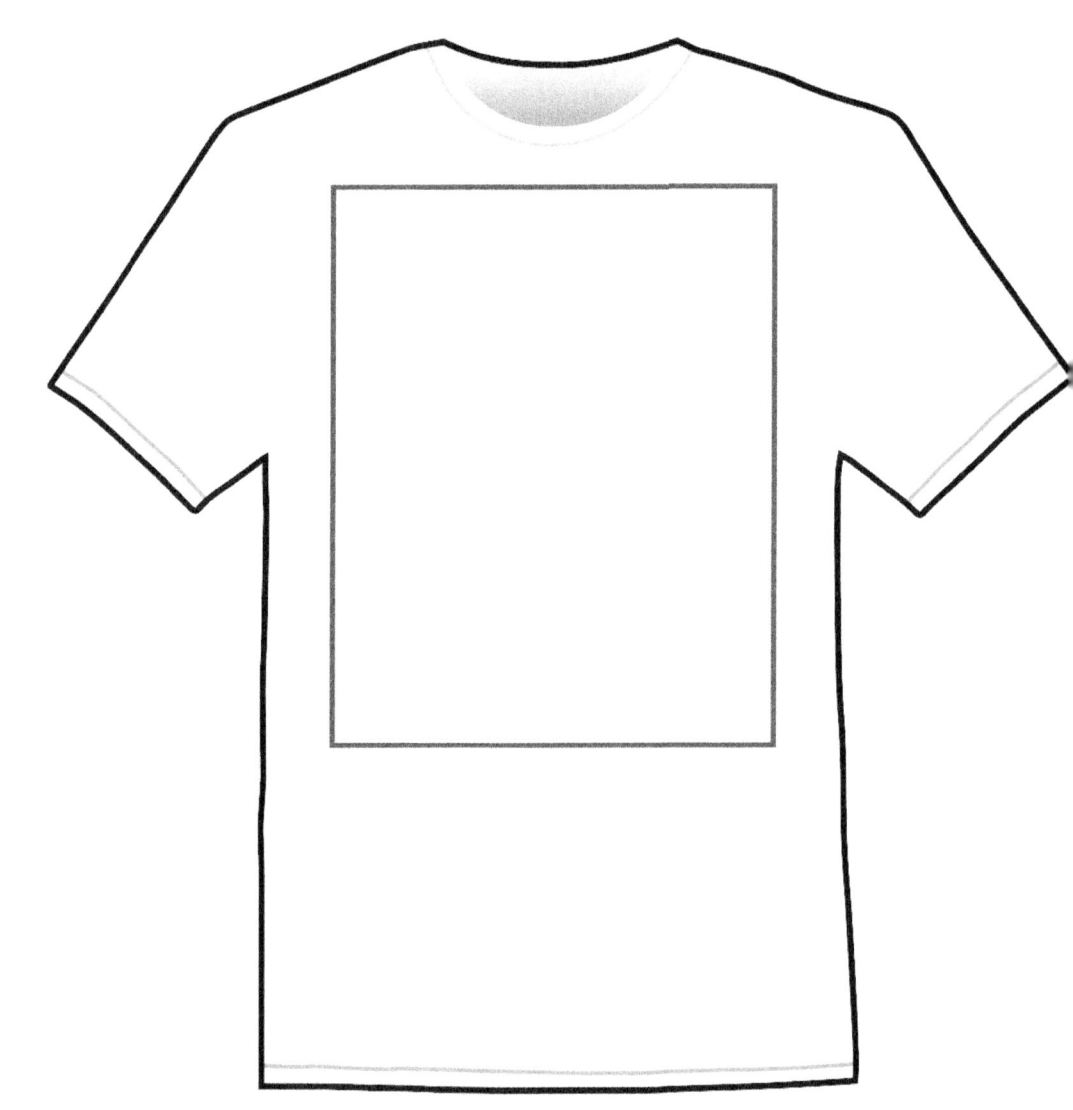

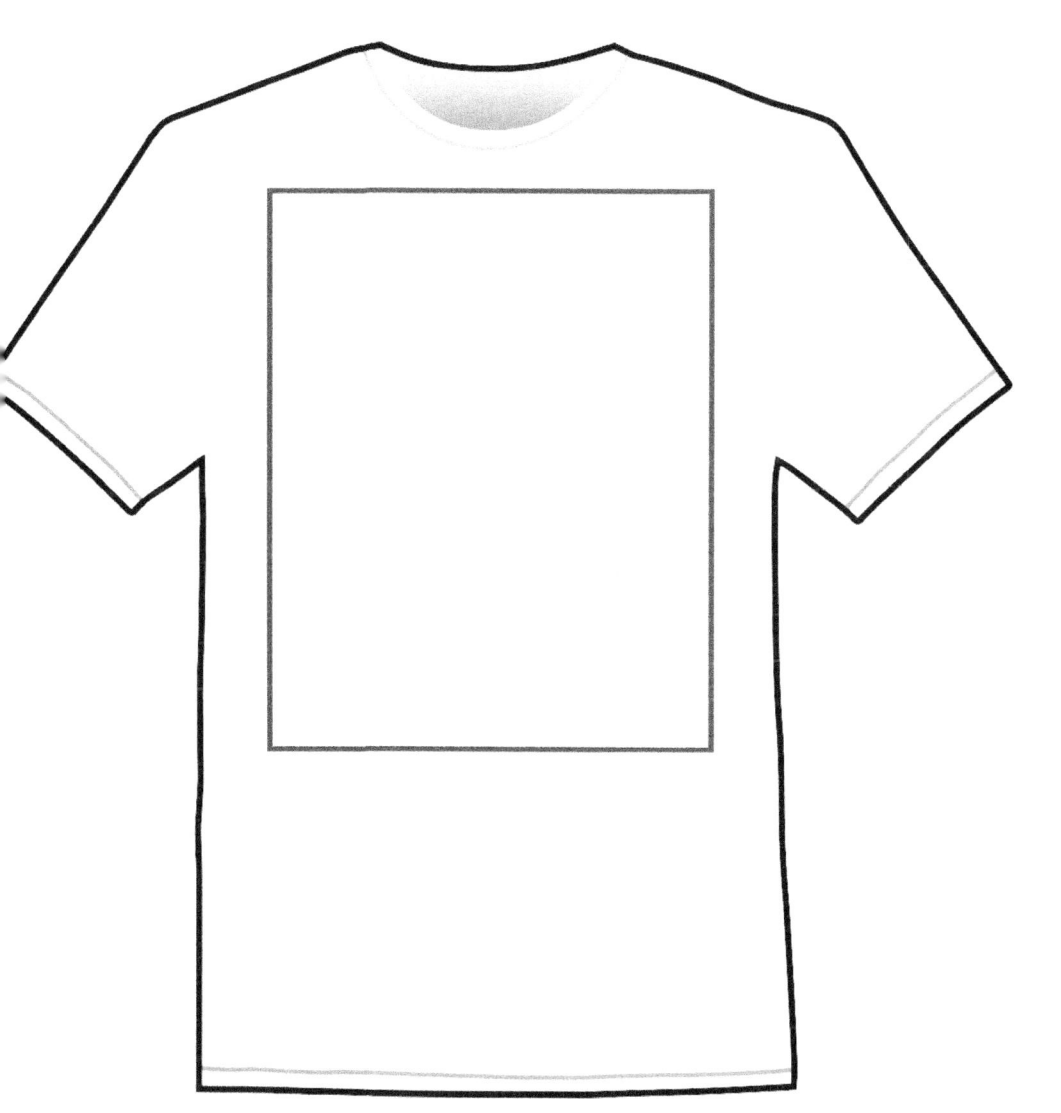

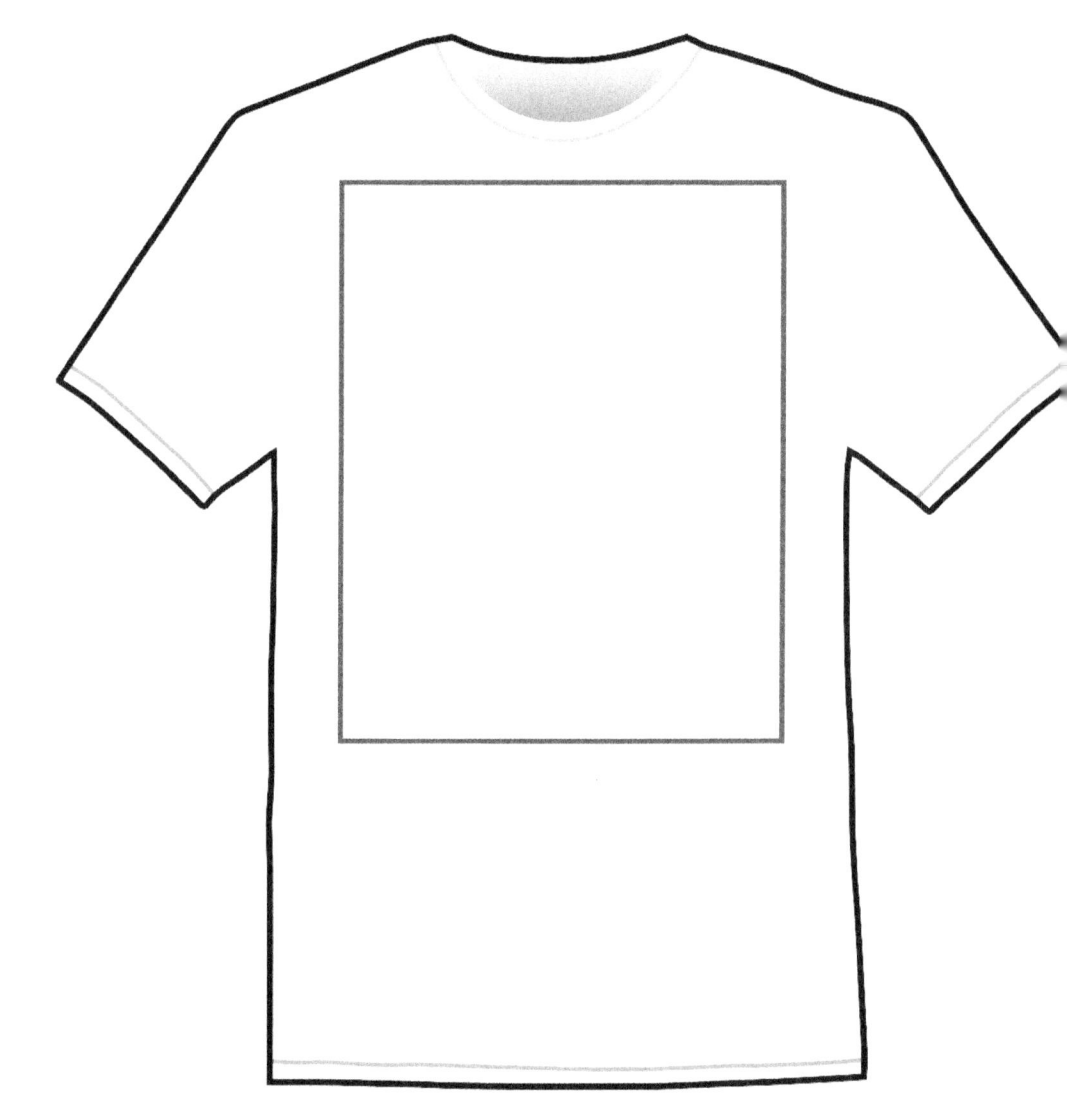

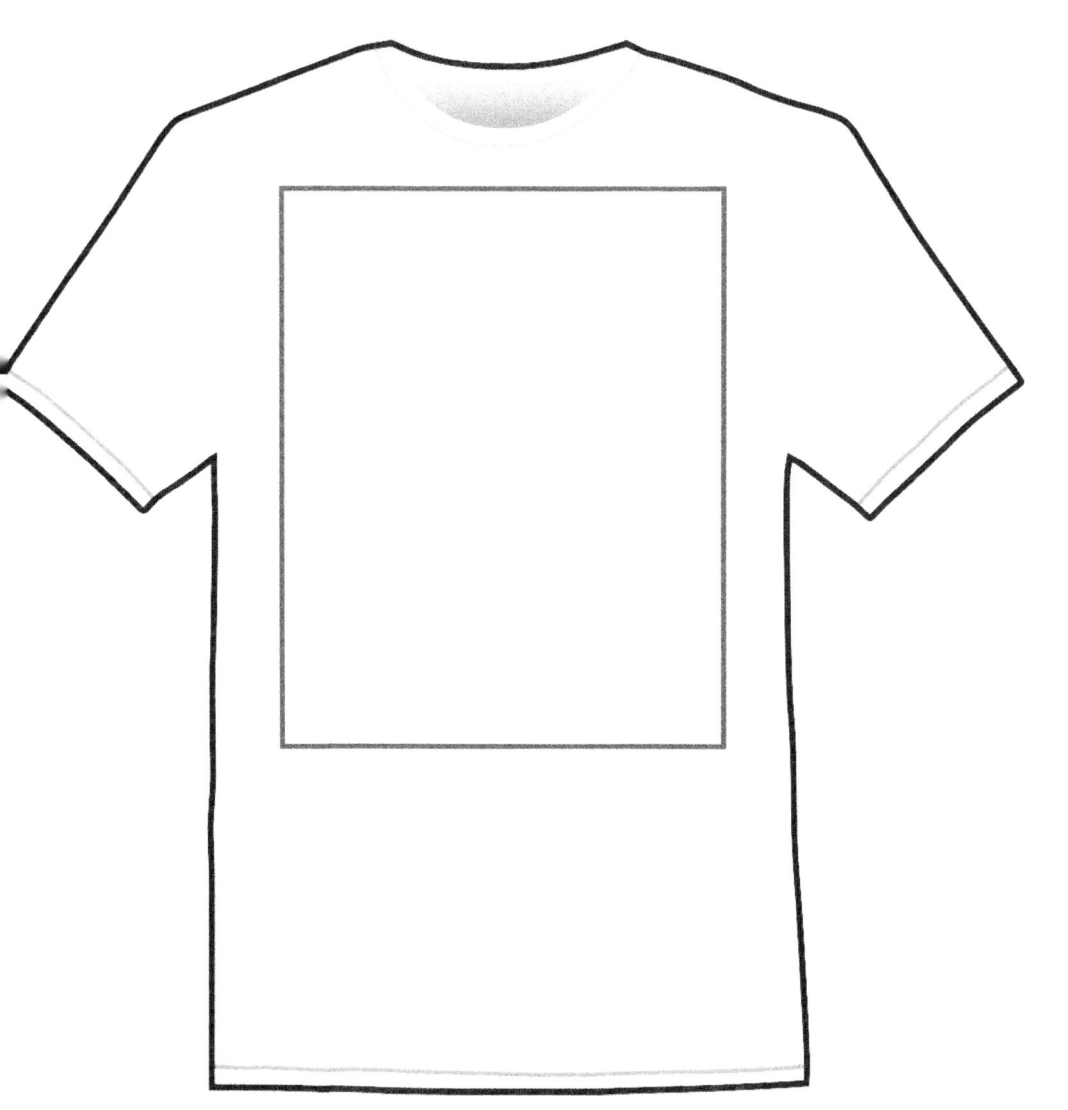

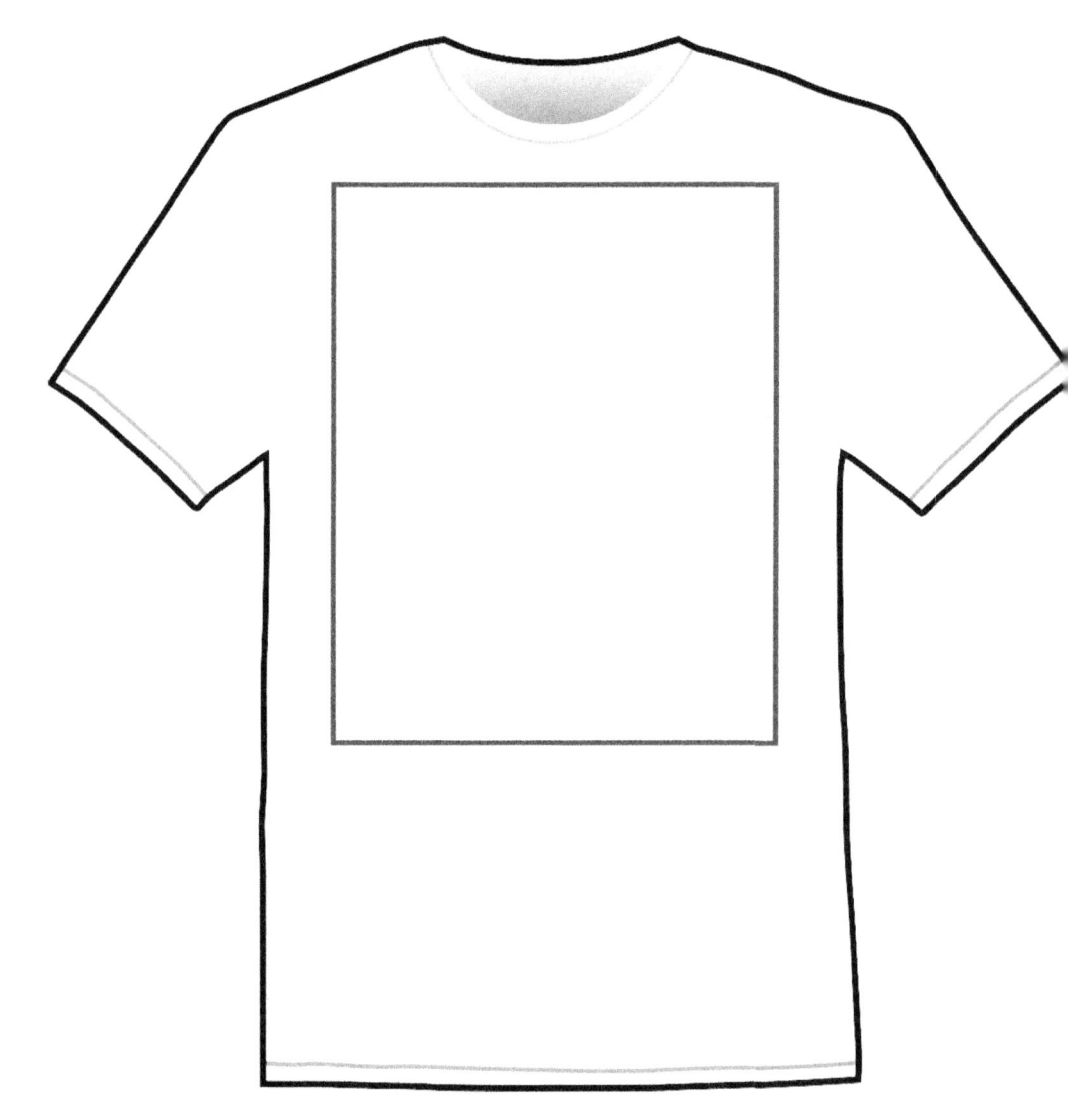

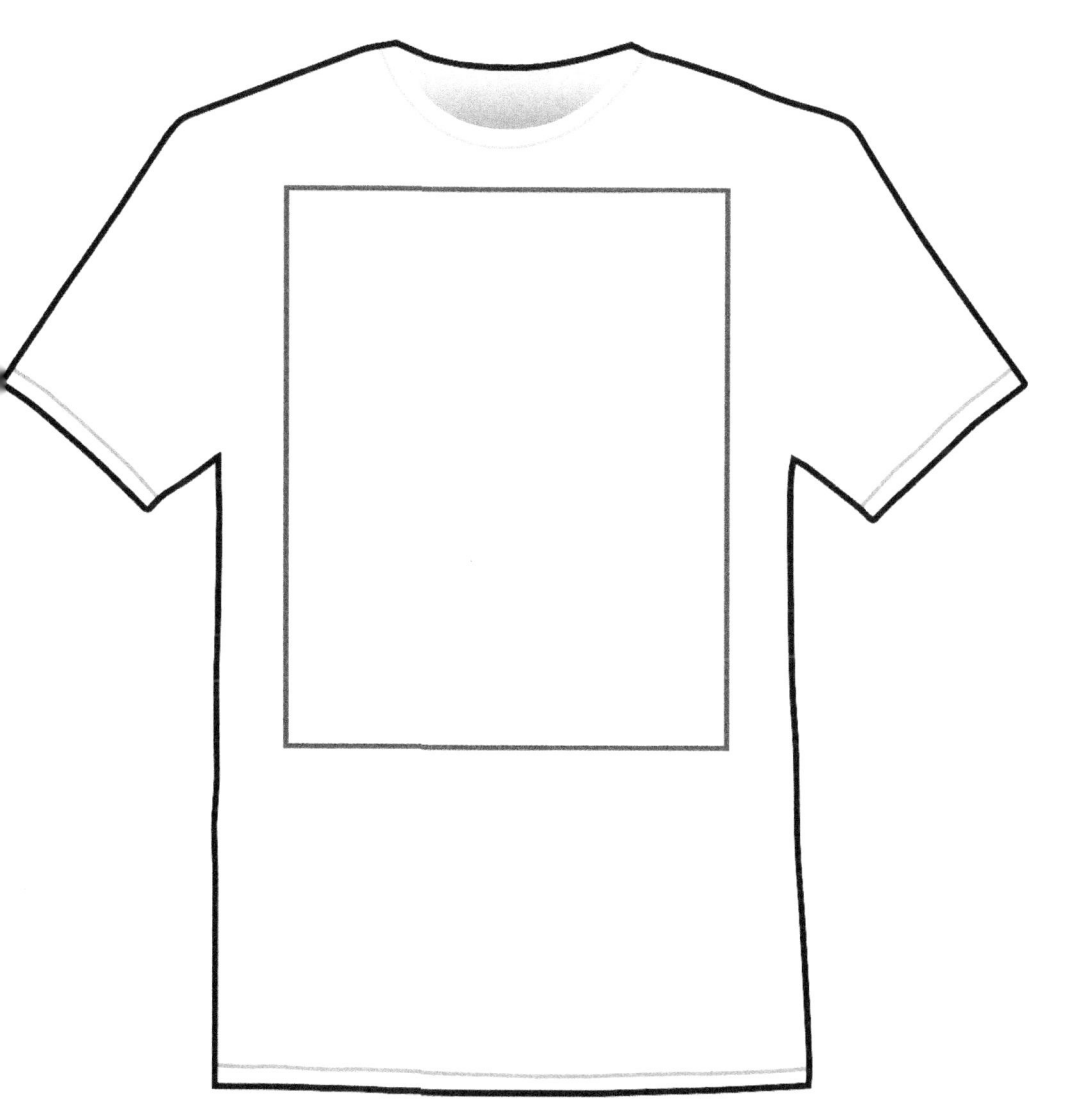

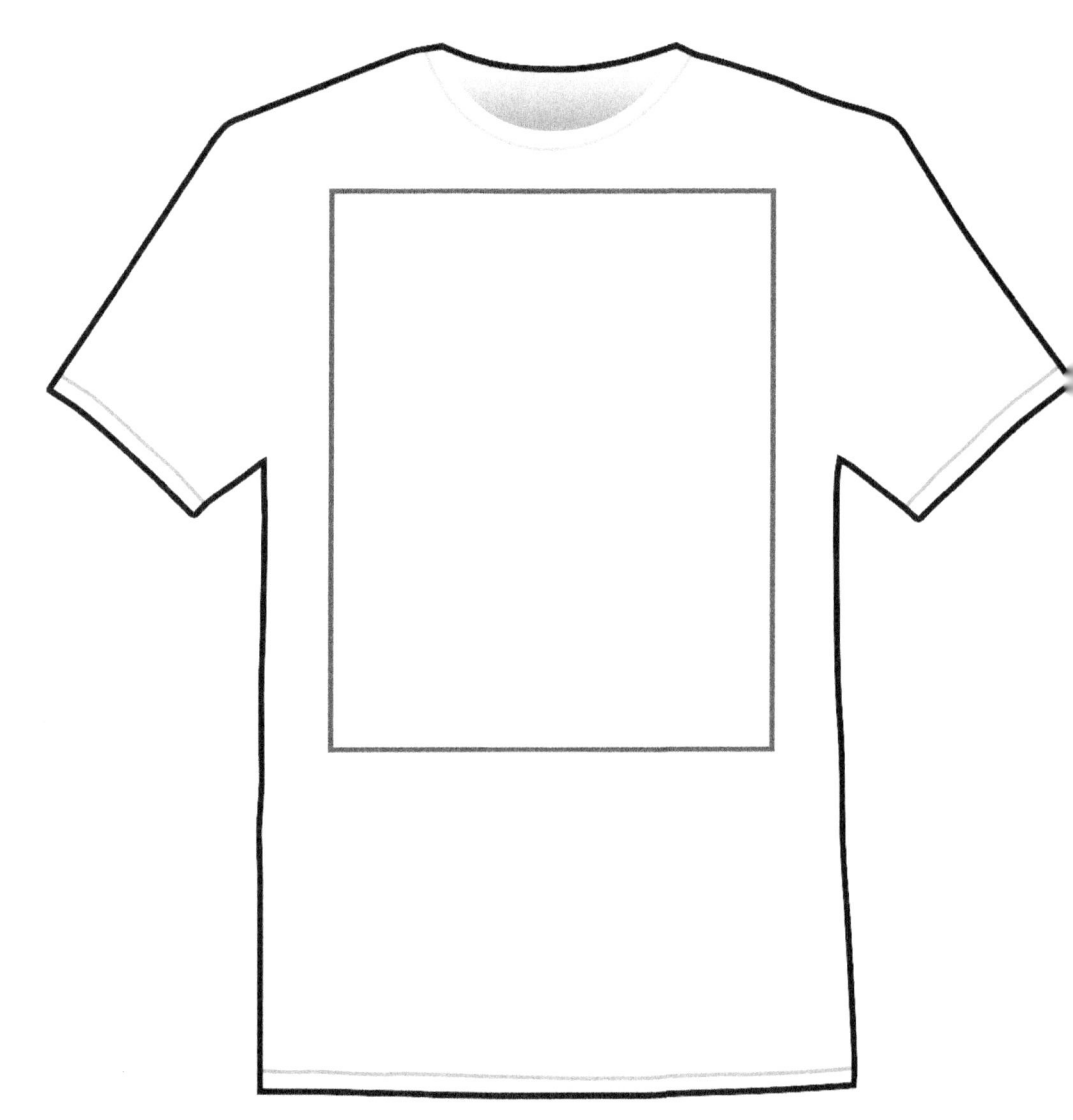

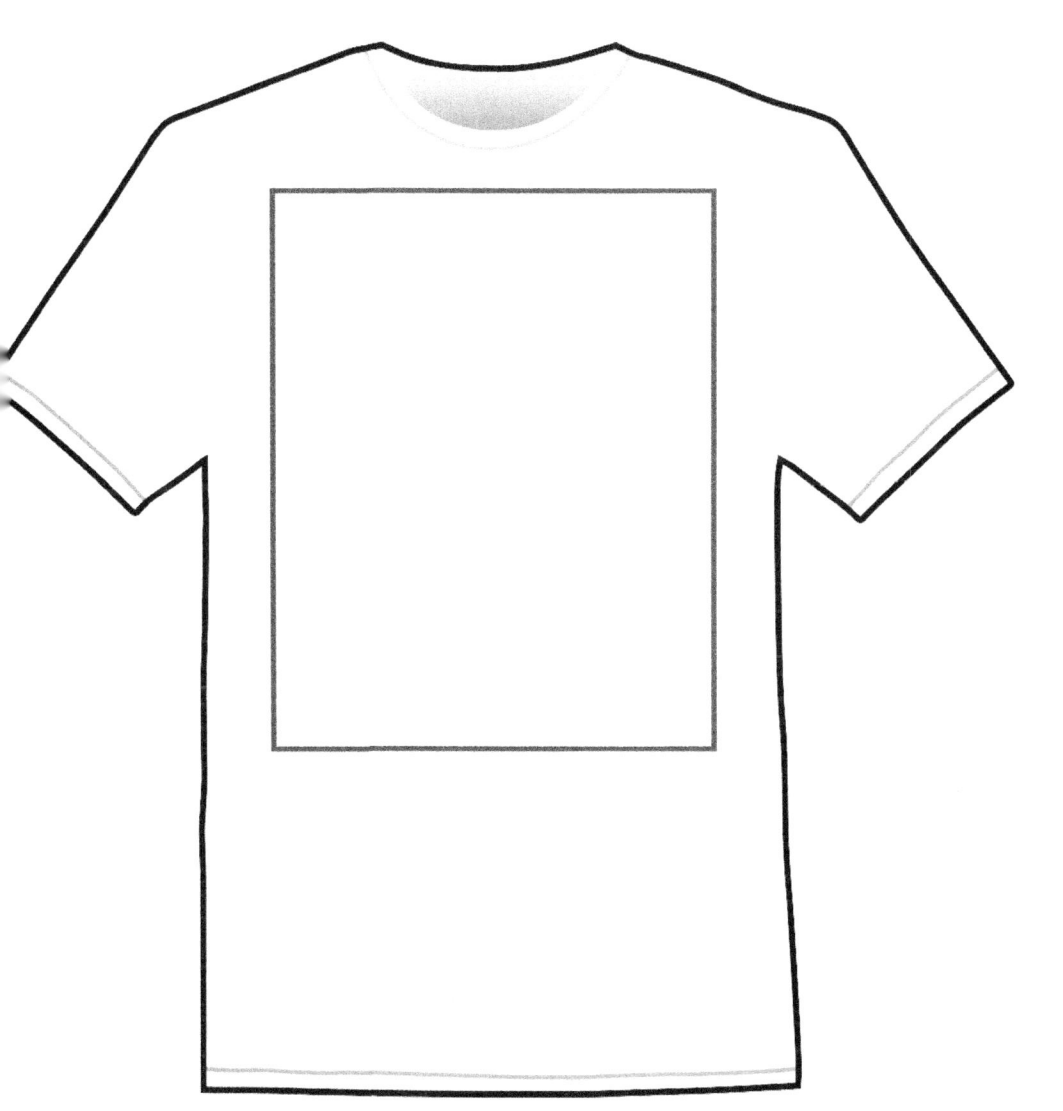

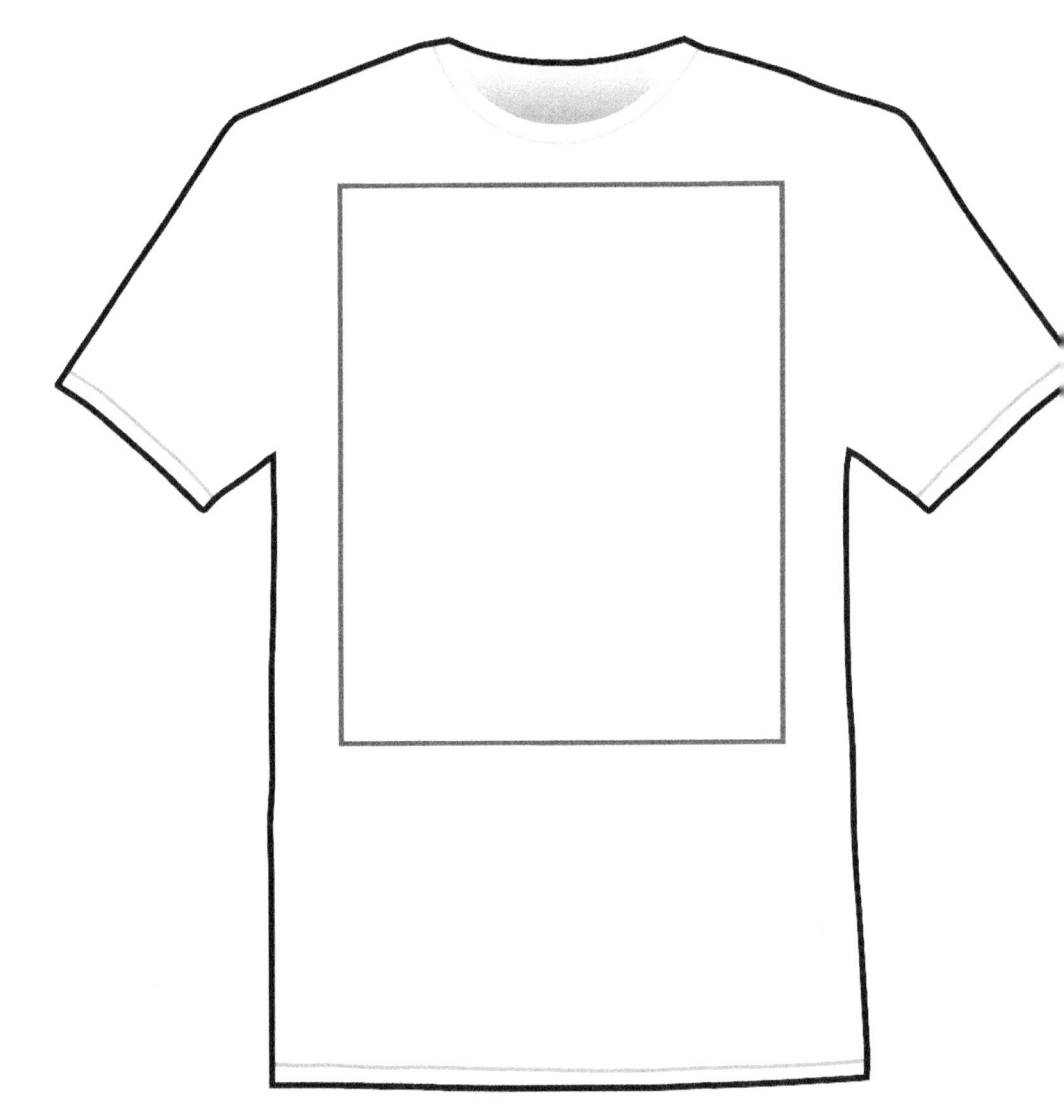

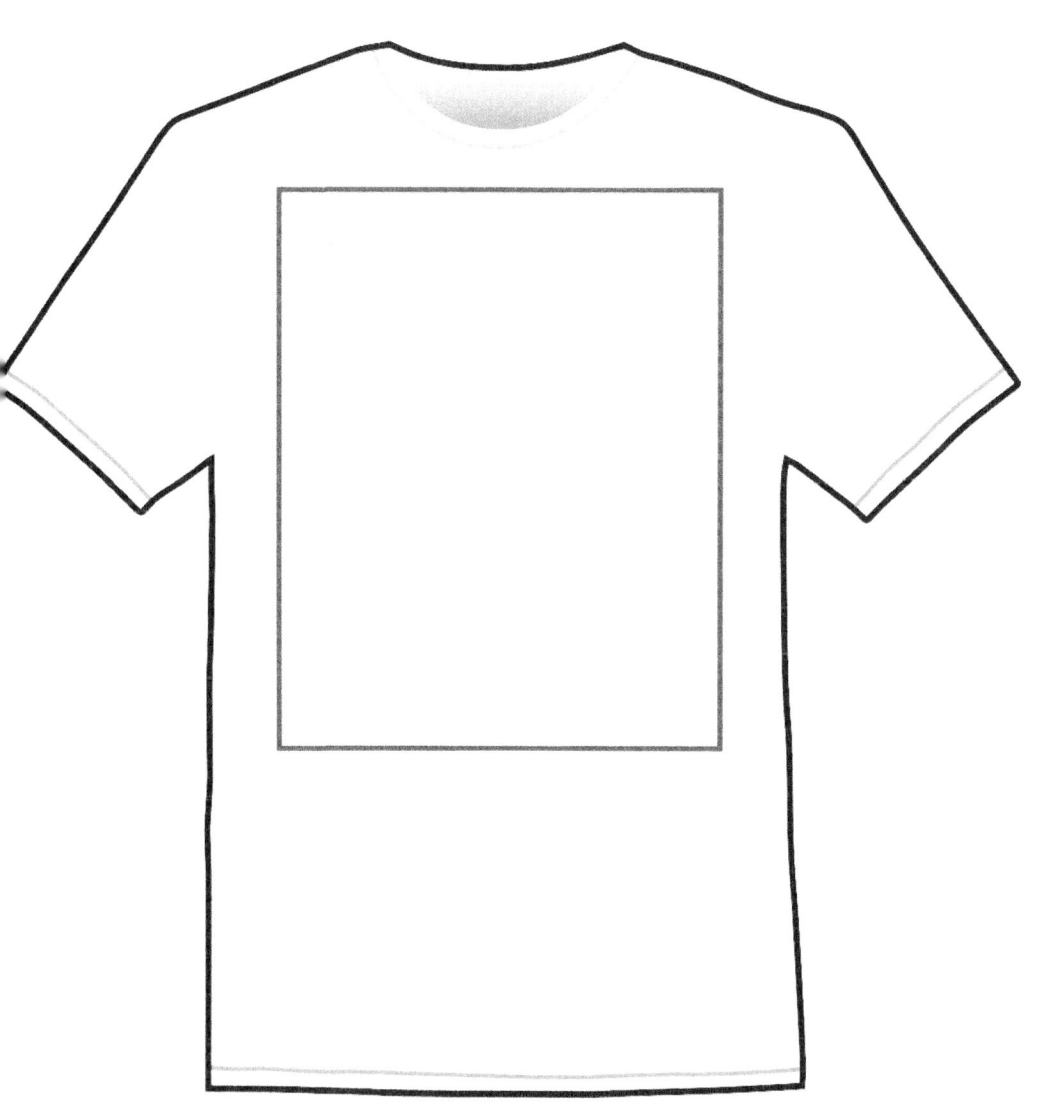

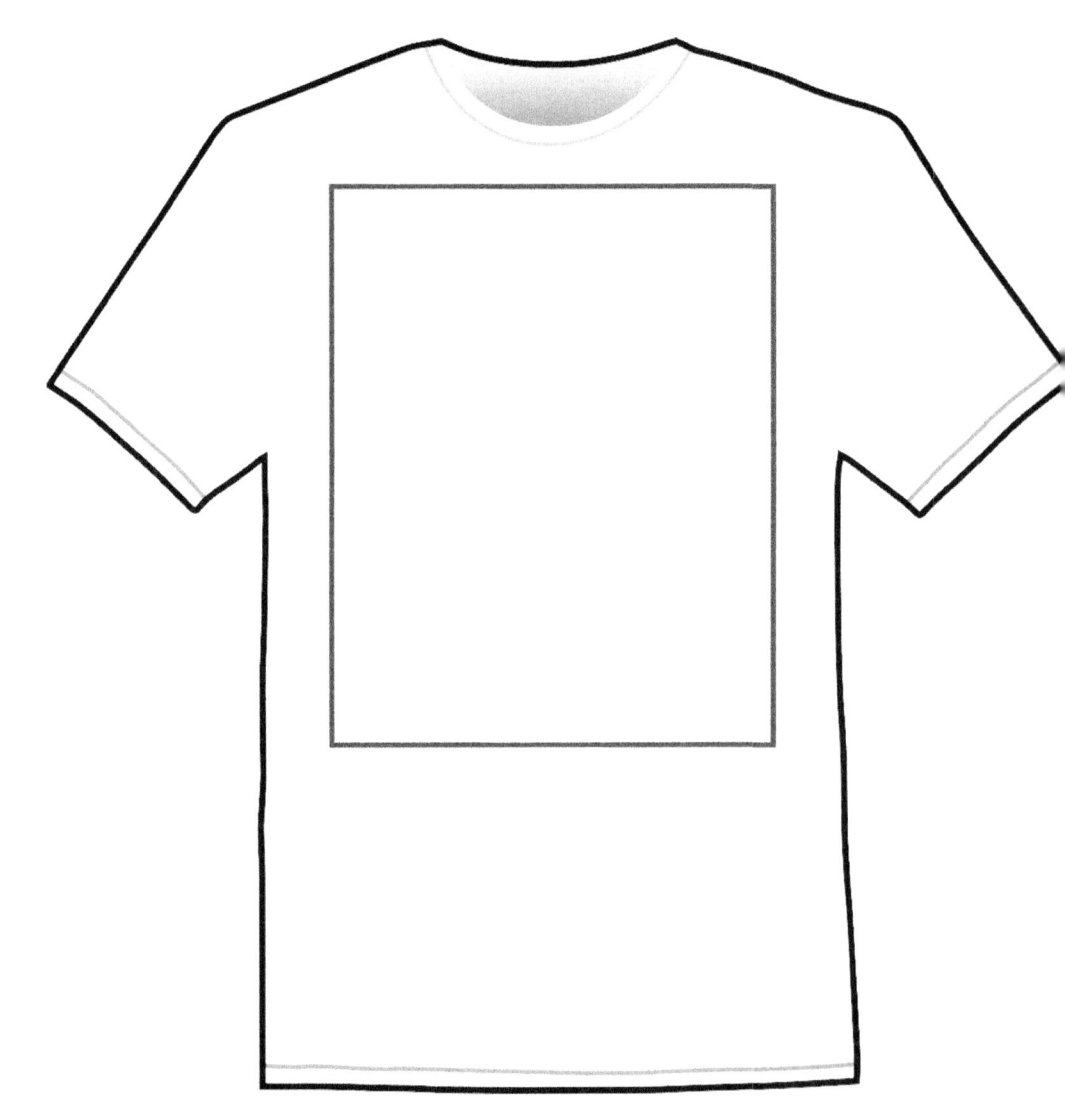

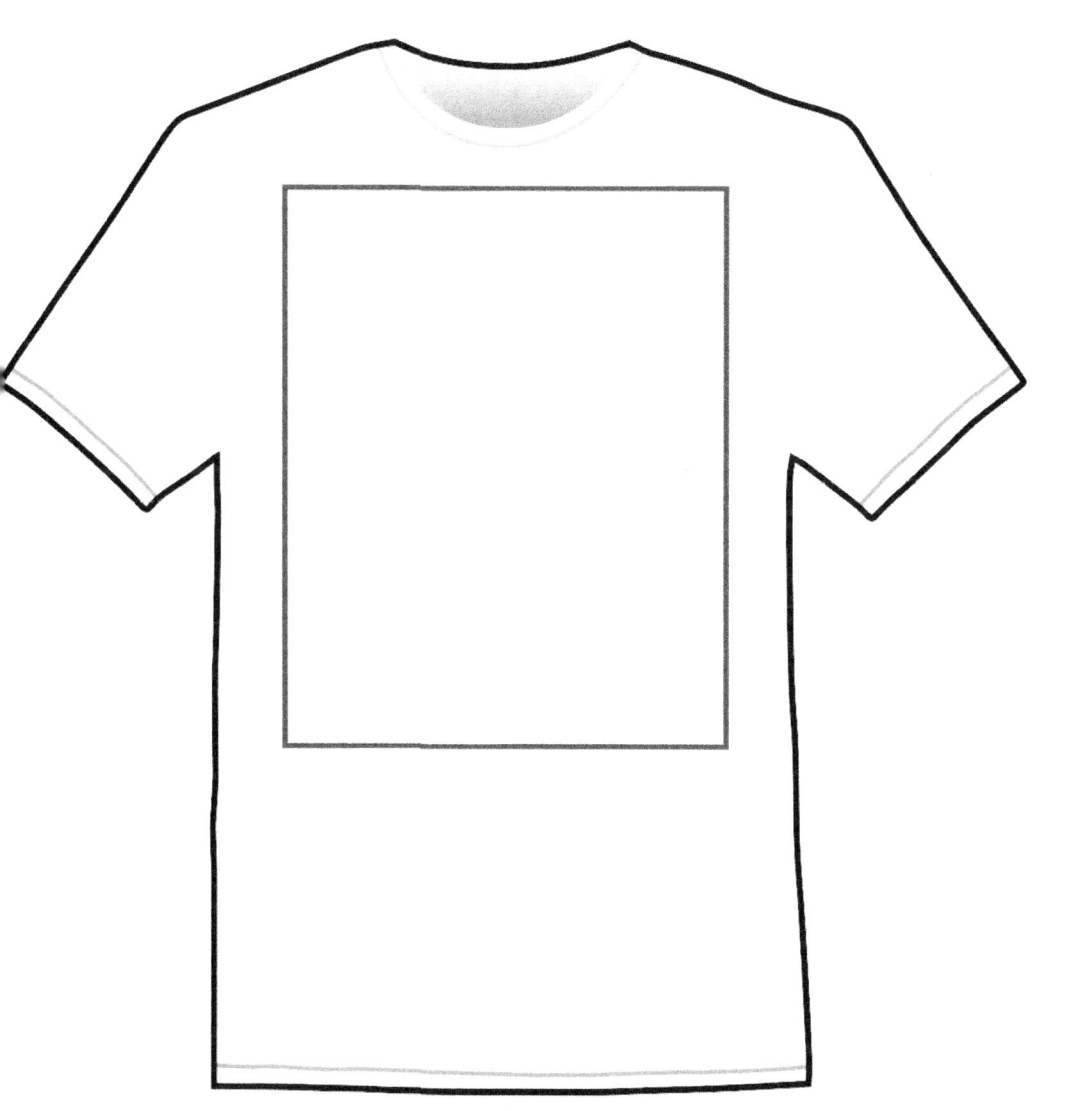

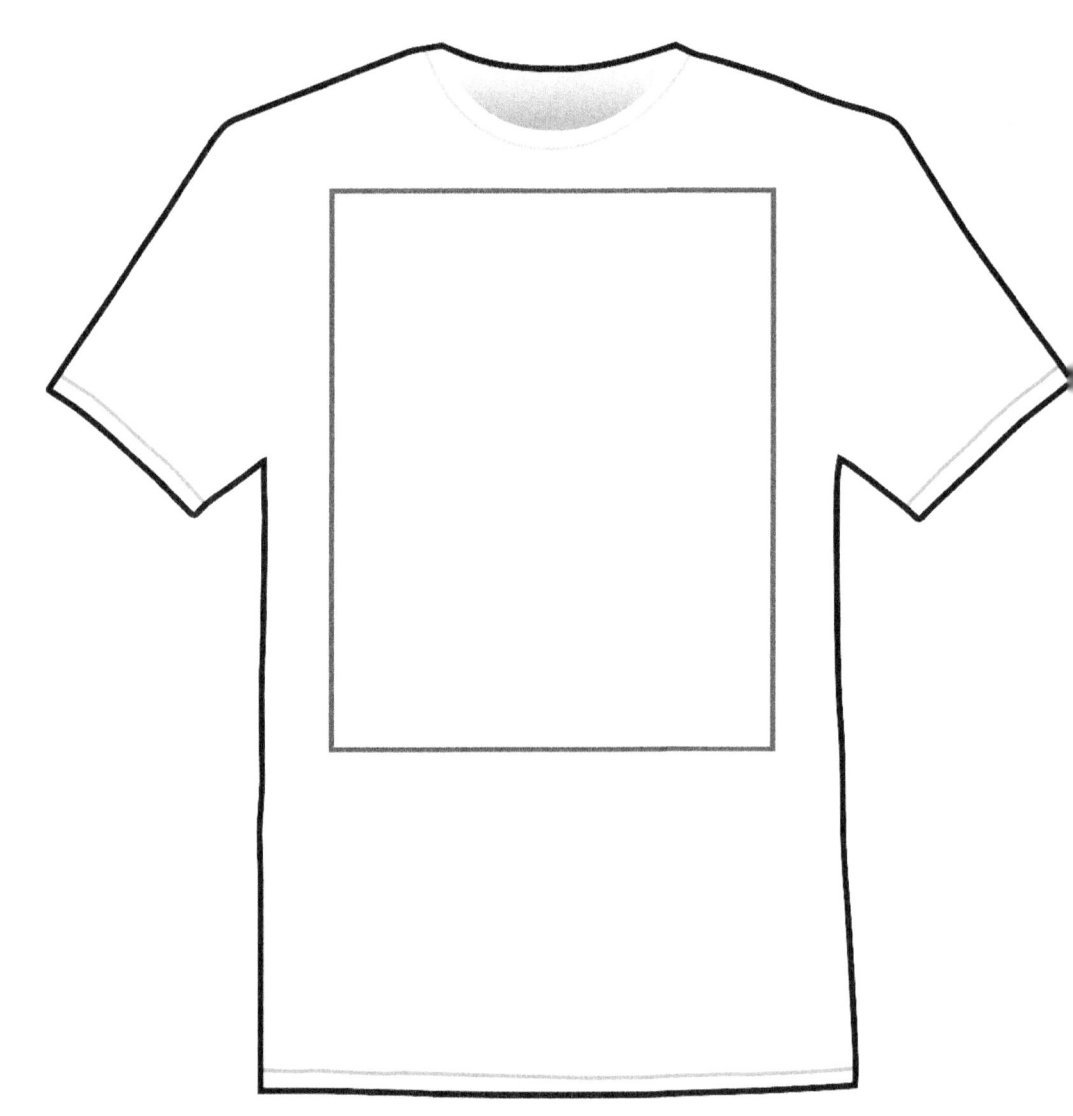

Merch By Amazon Resources:

MerchResearch.com
Search all Merch By Amazon designs by keyword as well as other print-on-demand sites, keyword tools, and more

MerchInformer.com
Simplified and streamlined Merch By Amazon research tool (use code chris20 to save 20% FOR LIFE)

Make-Merch.com
Pre-loaded with templates, filters, & artwork, Make-Merch makes making Merch By Amazon designs simple and easy

MerchDesigner.com/editor
FREE web-based designer for Merch By Amazon designs

DesignPickle.com
UNLIMITED graphic design requests for one monthly fee! Visit **MerchPickle.com** and use code CG2017 to save 30%!

Join the Facebook Group:
Facebook.com/groups/MerchLife
OR **www.merch.group**

Learn about Merch By Amazon with the Merch Life book:
Amazon.com/dp/1517795990

Merch By Amazon Udemy Courses
Udemy.com/merchbyamazonintro – Introduction
Udemy.com/merchbyamazon - Advanced

I hope that you find this sketchbook for Merch By Amazon useful!
Please let me know if I can help you in any way.

Message me through Facebook at:
facebook.com/chris
Or use this link: **m.me/chris**

Please also visit **ChrisGreen.com**

Find all of my books at:
Amazon.com/author/chris

Printed in Great Britain
by Amazon